THE PEOPLE'S REPUBLIC OF CHINA (PRC) continues to pursue a long-term, comprehensive military modernization program designed to improve the capacity of its armed forces to fight and win short-duration, high-intensity regional military conflict. Preparing for potential conflict in the Taiwan Strait appears to remain the principal focus and primary driver of China's military investment. However, as China's interests have grown and as it has gained greater influence in the international system, its military modernization has also become increasingly focused on investments in military capabilities to conduct a wider range of missions beyond its immediate territorial concerns, including counter-piracy, peacekeeping, humanitarian assistance/disaster relief, and regional military operations. Some of these missions and capabilities can address international security challenges, while others could serve more narrowly-defined PRC interests and objectives, including advancing territorial claims and building influence abroad.

To support the Chinese People's Liberation Army's (PLA) expanding set of roles and missions, China's leaders in 2012 sustained investment in advanced short- and medium-range conventional ballistic missiles, land-attack and anti-ship cruise missiles, counter-space weapons, and military cyberspace capabilities that appear designed to enable anti-access/area-denial (A2/AD) missions (what PLA strategists refer to as "counter-intervention operations"). The PLA also continued to improve capabilities in nuclear deterrence and long-range conventional strike; advanced fighter aircraft; limited regional power projection, with the commissioning of China's first aircraft carrier, the *Liaoning*; integrated air defenses; undersea warfare; improved command and control; and more sophisticated training and exercises across China's air, naval, and land forces.

During their January 2011 summit, U.S. President Barack Obama and then-PRC President Hu Jintao jointly affirmed that a "healthy, stable, and reliable military-to-military relationship is an essential part of [their] shared vision for a positive, cooperative, and comprehensive U.S.-China relationship." Within that framework, the U.S. Department of Defense seeks to build a military-to-military relationship with China that is sustained and substantive, while encouraging China to cooperate with the United States, our allies and partners, and the greater international community in the delivery of public goods. As the United States builds a stronger foundation for a military-to-military relationship with China, it also will continue to monitor China's evolving military strategy, doctrine, and force development and encourage China to be more transparent about its military modernization program. In concert with its allies and partners, the United States will continue adapting its forces, posture, and operational concepts to maintain a stable and secure Asia-Pacific security environment.

Contents

Executive Summary   i

Chapter 1: Annual Update   1

Chapter 2: Understanding China's Strategy   15

Chapter 3: Force Modernization Goals and Trends   29

Chapter 4: Resources for Force Modernization   45

Chapter 5: Force Modernization for a Taiwan Contingency   55

Chapter 6: U.S.-China Military-to-Military Contacts   61

Special Topic: Space-Based Imaging and Remote Sensing   65

Special Topic: China's First Aircraft Carrier   65

Special Topic: PLA Air Force Stealth Aircraft   66

Special Topic: PLA Integrated Air Defenses   67

Appendix I: Military-to-Military Exchanges   69

Appendix II: China and Taiwan Forces Data   75

Appendix III: Additional Maps and Chart   79

1
ANNUAL UPDATE

DEVELOPMENTS IN CHINA'S BILATERAL OR MULTILATERAL RELATIONSHIPS

China's military engagement with other countries seeks to enhance China's international presence and influence by improving relationships with foreign militaries, bolstering China's international and regional image, and assuaging other countries' concerns about China's rise. The People's Liberation Army's (PLA) engagement activities assist its modernization through the acquisition of advanced weapons systems and technologies, increased operational experience both throughout and beyond Asia, and access to foreign military practices, operational doctrine, and training methods.

In January 2013, China's Ministry of National Defense released information about the PLA's 2012 military diplomacy, which it stated had stood severe tests under a difficult international and regional situation throughout the year. In 2012, senior military officials from at least 25 countries visited China, including officials from Australia, Germany, Russia and Ukraine. Senior PLA officials visited at least 33 countries, including India, Poland, Tanzania, and Turkey. The PLA participated in UN peacekeeping operations (PKO), carried out humanitarian assistance and disaster relief work in Pakistan and conducted the second global goodwill voyage of the PLA Navy ZHENG HE training vessel. PLA leaders participated in various multilateral meetings, including the Defense Ministers' Meeting of the Shanghai Cooperation Organization (SCO) and the Association of Southeast Asian Nations (ASEAN) Regional Forum Security Policy Conference.

Combined Exercises. PLA participation in bilateral and multilateral exercises is increasing. The PLA derives political benefit through increased influence and enhanced ties with partner states and organizations. Such exercises provide the PLA opportunities to improve capabilities and gain operational insights by observing tactics, command decision-making, and equipment used by more advanced militaries.

In 2011 and 2012 alone, the PLA held 21 joint exercise and training events with foreign militaries, compared to 32 during the entire 11th Five-Year Plan period (2006-2010). These activities included military exercises with SCO members, naval exercises, ground forces training, peacekeeping, and search and rescue operations/missions. China also conducted joint training for operations other than war, including the 2011 COOPERATION SPIRIT humanitarian assistance/disaster relief (HA/DR) exercise with Australia. China observed KHAN QUEST-11, a peacekeeping exercise in Mongolia – the first time it had done so. The PLA Navy conducted maritime exercises with Russia, Vietnam, and Thailand

and counter-piracy exercises with France and the United States.

The PLA Air Force (PLAAF) conducted unprecedented bilateral training during 2011, including its first bilateral air exercise with Pakistan and training with air forces in Belarus and Venezuela. In contrast, the PLA Air Force participated in only one bilateral exercise in 2012 – an airborne training exercise with Belarus in November. PEACE MISSION 2012, conducted under the auspices of the SCO, did not include PLA Air Force participation as in the past, and instead focused on what SCO nations called "counterterrorism" training, which more closely resembles training to suppress armed opposition within a member country.

Peacekeeping Operations (PKO).

Over the past ten years, China has increased its commitment to UN PKO by approximately ten fold, building to its current level of approximately 2,000 personnel in 11 operations, mostly in sub-Saharan Africa and the Middle East. This level of support has been steadily maintained since 2008 and is the highest among the permanent members of the UN Security Council. In total, China has deployed more than 21,000 troops to 30 UN missions and bears 3.93 percent of the UN's current peacekeeping budget of $7.23 billion.

PKO participation can serve various objectives, including improving China's international image, obtaining operational experience, providing opportunities to gather intelligence, and advancing the PLA's "New Historic Missions" by taking on roles and generating capabilities for operations far beyond China's borders. China is currently taking steps to meet these objectives by committing civilian police, military observers, engineers, logistics support, and medical troops to UN missions while abstaining from missions that might result in regime change or lack host country consent.

In 2012, China for the first time deployed infantry to a UN PKO. This "guard unit," as Chinese media described it, is tasked with security for the PLA engineering and medical formed military units in its contingent deployed to the United Nations Mission in the Republic of South Sudan (UNMISS). These forces, likely no more than 50 personnel from the 162nd Motorized Infantry Division, are equipped with armored vehicles, enabling them to provide fixed-site security and convoy escorts.

Chinese Arms Sales.

From 2007 to 2011, Chinese arms sales totaled approximately $11 billion. As of this report's publication, data for 2012 arms sales was not yet available. China primarily conducts arms sales in conjunction with economic aid and development assistance to support broader foreign-policy goals such as securing access to natural resources and export markets, promoting its increasing political influence among host-country elites, and building support in international forums. Arms sales, however, also can reflect the profit-seeking activities of individual arms trading companies and efforts to offset defense-related research and development costs. For example, China continues to develop and market unmanned aerial vehicles (UAVs) abroad, and in 2012, unveiled a new tactical UAV, the Yi Long, which will likely be marketed to developing countries.

From the perspective of China's arms customers (most of whom are developing countries), Chinese arms are less expensive than those offered by the top international arms suppliers, although they are also generally of lower quality and reliability. Chinese arms also come with fewer political strings attached, which is attractive to those customers who may not have access to other sources of arms for political or economic reasons. China also offers relatively generous terms and flexible payment options to some customers.

Counter-Piracy Efforts. China continues to support counter-piracy efforts in the Gulf of Aden, a commitment which began in December 2008. In July 2012, the PLA Navy deployed its 12th escort formation, which included two guided missile frigates and one oiler. Operational highlights for this formation included the retrieval of 26 crew members of the fishing vessel Xufu-1 from Somalia following their release by pirates in July 2012 (an operation that was recognized

by China's Central Military Commission); and the first combined counter-piracy exercise with the U.S. Navy. After its departure from the Gulf of Aden, the 11th escort formation visited Ukraine and Turkey, and for the first time for the PLA Navy, Romania, Bulgaria and Israel. Ships engaged in counter-piracy also conducted port calls in Australia, Mozambique, and Thailand during 2012.

Territorial Disputes. Senior Chinese officials have identified protecting China's sovereignty and territorial integrity as a "core interest" and all officials repeatedly state China's opposition to and willingness to respond to actions it perceives as challenging this core interest. In 2012, this was demonstrated by Chinese actions at Scarborough Reef in the South China Sea and the Senkaku Islands in the East China Sea.

The Chinese government maintains that its maritime rights extend to virtually the entire South China Sea and often illustrates this claim using a "nine-dash line" that encompasses much of the South China Sea area. At the same time, Beijing is ambiguous about the precise meaning of the nine-dash line; to date, China has not clarified the meaning of the nine-dash line or its legal basis. In April 2012, Chinese maritime law enforcement vessels and Philippine coast guard vessels engaged in a protracted standoff at Scarborough Reef, after the Philippine Navy attempted to conduct a fishing enforcement action against Chinese fishermen.

Although overt tensions between China and the Philippines subsided by year's end, both sides continue to claim jurisdiction over the reef. Chinese law enforcement vessels have maintained an almost continuous presence ever since.

In November 2012, China also added a map which contained the nine-dash line to all of its new passports. This action elicited negative responses from other nations in the Asia-Pacific region. China's increased reference in official government materials to the nine-dash line is a source of concern to its neighbors and other nations because, at a minimum, it creates an impression that China is not merely claiming all the land features within the nine-dash line, but it may also be claiming a special sovereign status of all the water and the sea-bed contained therein.

China claims sovereignty over the Senkaku Islands (what the Chinese refer to as the Diaoyu Islands) in the East China Sea, territory also claimed by Taiwan and Japan. In April 2012, the Governor of Tokyo announced plans to purchase three of the five islets from private Japanese owners. In response, in September 2012, the Government of Japan purchased the three islands. China protested the move and since that time has regularly sent maritime law enforcement ships (and, less often, aircraft) to patrol near the Senkakus to protect its claims; this has included regular Chinese maritime operations within 12nm of the islands. On September 25, China published a white paper entitled, "Diaoyu Dao, an 'Inherent Territory' of China." In addition, in September 2012, China began using improperly drawn straight baseline claims around the Senkaku Islands, adding to its network of maritime claims inconsistent with international law. In December 2012, China submitted information to the U.N. Commission on the Limits of the Continental Shelf regarding China's extended continental shelf in the East China Sea that includes the disputed islands.

THE SECURITY SITUATION IN THE TAIWAN STRAIT

Dealing with a potential contingency in the Taiwan Strait remains the PLA's primary mission despite decreasing tensions there - a trend which continued following the re-election of Taiwan President Ma Ying-jeou in January 2012. In this context, should deterrence fail, the PLA could be called upon to compel Taiwan to abandon independence or to re-unify with the mainland by force of arms while defeating any third-party intervention on Taiwan's behalf.

Cross-Strait Stability. China and Taiwan have reached 18 agreements for cross-Strait cooperation on economic, cultural, and functional issues, but Taiwan authorities and the broader Taiwan public do not support negotiation on issues directly related to sovereignty.

China and Taiwan have also undertaken some combined security and police operations, and held a combined maritime rescue exercise in August 2012 featuring two helicopters, 14 vessels, and 300 personnel, with both sides equally represented. Also in August, Chinese and Taiwan police apprehended 30 suspects in a human-trafficking and prostitution ring – a first collaborative effort to combat human trafficking.

During a mid-October 2011 speech, President Ma stated that a cross-Strait peace agreement with China might be attainable in 10 years, but backed down immediately in the face of widespread negative public reaction and Ma specified the conditions under which he would pursue such an agreement. Despite occasional signs of impatience, China appears content to respect Taiwan's current approach to cross-Strait relations. In November 2012, Xi Jinping, China's newly selected general secretary of the CCP Central Committee sent a message to President Ma (in the latter's capacity as chairman of the ruling Kuomintang Party), emphasizing the need to continue promoting the peaceful development of cross-Strait relations. This early message suggests that China under Xi Jinping may be willing to follow President Hu Jintao's multi-pronged strategy for developing cross-Strait relations rather than compelling unification through the use of force. President Hu in his report to the 18th Party Congress in November 2012 used language that promoted

peaceful reunification and called for both sides to explore political relations and make reasonable arrangements to discuss the creation of a military confidence-building mechanism.

CURRENT CAPABILITIES OF THE PEOPLE'S LIBERATION ARMY

Second Artillery. The Second Artillery controls China's nuclear and conventional ballistic missiles. It is developing and testing several new classes and variants of offensive missiles, forming additional missile units, upgrading older missile systems, and developing methods to counter ballistic missile defenses.

By December 2012, the Second Artillery's inventory of short-range ballistic missiles (SRBM) deployed to units opposite Taiwan stood at more than 1,100. This number reflects the delivery of additional missiles and the fielding of new systems. To improve the lethality of this force, the PLA is also introducing new SRBM variants with improved ranges, accuracies, and payloads.

China is fielding a limited but growing number of conventionally armed, medium-range ballistic missiles, including the DF-21D anti-ship ballistic missile (ASBM). The DF-21D is based on a variant of the DF-21 (CSS-5) medium-range ballistic missile (MRBM) and gives the PLA the capability to attack large ships, including aircraft carriers, in the western Pacific Ocean. The DF-21D has a range exceeding 1,500 km and is armed with a maneuverable warhead.

The Second Artillery continues to modernize its nuclear forces by enhancing its silo-based intercontinental ballistic missiles (ICBMs) and adding more survivable mobile delivery systems. In recent years, the road-mobile, solid-propellant CSS-10 Mod 1 and CSS-10 Mod 2 (DF-31 and DF-31A) intercontinental-range ballistic missiles have entered service. The CSS-10 Mod 2, with a range in excess of 11,200 km, can reach most locations within the continental United States. China may also be developing a new road-mobile ICBM, possibly capable of carrying a multiple independently targetable re-entry vehicle (MIRV).

PLA Navy (PLAN). The PLA Navy has the largest force of major combatants, submarines, and amphibious warfare ships in Asia. China's naval forces include some 79 principal surface combatants, more than 55 submarines, 55 medium and large amphibious ships, and roughly 85 missile-equipped small combatants.

In the most publicized PLA Navy modernization event of 2012, after a year of extensive sea trials, China commissioned its first aircraft carrier, the *Liaoning,* in September 2012. The PLA Navy successfully conducted its first launch and recovery of the carrier-capable J-15 fighter on November 26, 2012.

The *Liaoning* will continue integration testing and training with the aircraft during the next several years, but it is not expected to embark an operational air wing until 2015 or later. China also continues to pursue an indigenous aircraft carrier program (the *Liaoning* is a refurbished vessel, purchased from Ukraine in 1998), and will likely build multiple aircraft carriers over the next decade. The first Chinese-built carrier will likely be operational sometime in the second half of this decade.

The PLA Navy places a high priority on the modernization of its submarine force. China continues the production of JIN-class nuclear-powered ballistic missile submarines (SSBN). Three JIN-class SSBNs (Type 094) are currently operational, and up to five may enter service before China proceeds to its next generation SSBN (Type 096) over the next decade. The JIN-class SSBN will carry the new JL-2 submarine launched ballistic missile with an estimated range of more than 4,000 nm. The JIN-class and the JL-2 will give the PLA Navy its first credible sea-based nuclear deterrent.

China also has expanded its force of nuclear-powered attack submarines (SSN). Two SHANG-class SSNs (Type 093) are already in service, and China is building four improved variants of the SHANG-class SSN, which will replace the aging HAN-class SSNs (Type 091). In the next decade, China will likely construct the Type 095 guided-missile attack submarine (SSGN), which may enable a submarine-based land-attack capability. In addition to likely incorporating better quieting technologies, the Type 095 will fulfill traditional anti-ship roles with the incorporation of torpedoes and anti-ship cruise missiles (ASCMs).

The current mainstay of the Chinese submarine force is modern diesel powered attack submarines (SS). In addition to 12 KILO-class submarines acquired from Russia in the 1990s and 2000s (eight of which are equipped with the SS-N-27 ASCM), the PLA Navy possesses 13 SONG-class SS (Type 039) and eight YUAN-class SSP (Type 039A). The YUAN-class SSP is armed similarly to the SONG-class SS, but also includes an air-independent power system. China may plan to construct up to 20 YUAN-class SSPs.

Since 2008, the PLA Navy has embarked on a robust surface combatant construction program of various classes of ships, including guided missile destroyers (DDG) and guided missile frigates (FFG). During 2012, China continued series production of several classes, including construction of a new generation of DDG. Construction of the LUYANG II-class DDG (Type 052C) continued, with one ship entering service in 2012, and an additional three ships under various stages of construction and sea trials, bringing the total number of ships of this class to six by the end of 2013. Additionally, China launched the lead ship in a follow-on class, the LUYANG III- class DDG (Type 052D), which will likely enter service in 2014. The LUYANG III incorporates the PLA Navy's first multipurpose vertical launch system, likely capable of launching ASCM, land attack cruise missiles (LACM), surface-to-air missiles (SAM), and anti-submarine rockets. China is projected to build more than a dozen of these ships to replace its aging LUDA-class destroyers (DD). China has continued the construction of the workhorse JIANGKAI II-class FFG (Type 054A), with 12 ships currently in the fleet and six or more in various stages of construction, and yet more expected. These new DDGs and FFGs provide a significant upgrade to the PLA Navy's area air defense capability, which will be critical as it expands operations into "distant seas" beyond the range of shore-based air defense.

Augmenting the PLA Navy's littoral warfare capabilities, especially in the South China Sea and East China Sea, is a new class of small combatant. At least six of the JIANGDAO-class corvettes (FFL) (Type 056) were launched in 2012. The first of these ships entered service on February 25, 2013; China may build 20 to 30 of this class. These FFLs augment the 60 HOUBEI-class wave-piercing catamaran missile patrol boats (PTG) (Type 022), each capable of carrying eight YJ-83 ASCMs, for operations in littoral waters.

The PLA Navy also increased its amphibious force in 2012. Two YUZHAO-class amphibious transport docks (LPD) (Type

071) were accepted into service during the year bringing the total of YUZHAO LPDs to three.

PLA Air Force (PLAAF). China bases approximately 500 combat aircraft within unrefueled operational range of Taiwan and has the airfield capacity to expand that number by hundreds. China continues to field increasingly modern 4th generation aircraft, but the force still consists mostly of older 2nd and 3rd generation aircraft, or upgraded variants of those aircraft.

Within two years of the J-20 stealth fighter's first flight in January 2011, China tested a second next generation fighter prototype. The prototype, referred to as the "J-31," is similar in size to a U.S. F-35 fighter and appears to incorporate design characteristics similar to the J-20. It conducted its first flight on October 31, 2012.

China continues upgrading its H-6 bomber fleet (originally adapted from the late 1950s Soviet Tu-16 design) with a new variant that possesses greater range and will be armed with a long-range cruise missile. China also uses a modified version of the H-6 aircraft to conduct aerial refueling operations for many of its indigenous aircraft, increasing their combat range.

The PLA Air Force possesses one of the largest forces of advanced SAM systems in the world, consisting of a combination of Russian-sourced SA-20 battalions and domestically produced HQ-9 battalions.

China's aviation industry is developing a large transport aircraft (likely referred to as the Y-20) to supplement China's small fleet of strategic airlift assets, which currently consists of a limited number of Russian-made IL-76 aircraft. These heavy lift transports are needed to support airborne command and control (C2), logistics, paradrop, aerial refueling, and reconnaissance operations, as well as humanitarian assistance and disaster relief missions.

Developments in China's commercial and military aviation industry indicate improved aircraft manufacturing, associated technology, and systems development capabilities. Some of these advances have been made possible by business partnerships with Western aviation and aerospace firms (including cleared U.S. defense contractors), which provide overall benefit to China's military aerospace industry. China will continue to seek advancement in aerospace technology, capability, and proficiency to rival Western capabilities.

PLA Ground Force. The PLA is investing heavily in modernizing its ground force, emphasizing the ability to deploy campaign-level forces across long distances quickly. This modernization is playing out with wide-scale restructuring of PLA ground forces that includes a more rapid, flexible special operations force equipped with advanced technology; improved army aviation units utilizing ultra-low altitude mobility helicopters armed with precision-guided munitions; and command and control (C2) capabilities with improved networks providing real-time data transmissions within and between units. In addition, the PLA has focused its modernization efforts on transforming from a motorized to a mechanized force, as well as improving the ground force's armored, air defense, aviation, ground-air coordination, and electronic warfare (EW) capabilities. PLA ground forces have benefited from increased production of new equipment, including the Z-10 and Z-19 attack helicopters. New air defense equipment includes the PLA ground force's first medium-range SAM, the CSA-16, as well as domestically-produced CSA-15s (a copy of the Russian SA-15) and a new advanced self-propelled air defense artillery system, the PGZ-07. PLA ground force restructuring is highlighted by the development of brigades as a key operational echelon for combat in diverse terrain and under complex electromagnetic conditions.

The ground force is a proponent of joint operations since it requires transport from other forces to operate beyond China's borders. To assist with its power projection needs, PLA ground forces have practiced using commercial transport assets such as roll-on/roll-off ships, to conduct maritime crossing operations. However, broader joint operations capability are still the primary goal for the ground force, a goal that is now a mandate for all the military services following the General Staff Department's (GSD) December 2011 creation of the Military Training Department to oversee all PLA training, ensuring all military services realize the "prominence of joint training."

Space Capabilities. In 2012, China conducted 18 space launches. China also expanded its space-based intelligence, surveillance, reconnaissance, navigation, meteorological, and communications satellite constellations. In parallel, China is developing a multi-dimensional program to improve its capabilities to limit or prevent the use of space-based assets by adversaries during times of crisis or conflict.

During 2012, China launched six Beidou navigation satellites. These six satellites completed the regional network as well as the in-orbit validation phase for the global network, expected to be completed by 2020. China launched 11 new remote sensing satellites in 2012, which can perform both civil and military applications. China also launched three communications satellites, five experimental small satellites, one meteorological satellite, one relay satellite, and a manned space mission.

China continues to develop the Long March 5 (LM-5) rocket, which is intended to lift heavy payloads into space. LM-5 will more than double the size of the Low Earth Orbit

(LEO) and Geosynchronous Orbit (GEO) payloads China is capable of placing into orbit. To support these rockets, China began constructing the Wenchang Satellite Launch Center in 2008. Located on Hainan Island, this launch facility is expected to be complete around 2013, with the initial LM-5 launch scheduled for 2014.

Military Information Operations. Chinese writings have outlined the five key features at an operational level of a maturing Chinese information operations (IO) strategy. First, Chinese authors emphasize defense as the top priority and indicate that Computer Network Defense (CND) must be the highest priority in peacetime; Chinese doctrine suggests that "tactical counteroffensives" would only be considered if an adversary's operations could not be countered. Second, IO is viewed as an unconventional warfare weapon, which must be established in the opening phase of the conflict and continue during all phases of war. Third, IO is characterized as a preemption weapon to be used under the rubric of achieving information dominance and controlling the electromagnetic spectrum. Fourth, IO is seen as a tool to permit China to fight and win an information campaign, precluding the need for conventional military action. Fifth, potential Chinese adversaries, in particular the United States, are seen as "information dependent."

An IO campaign includes actions taken to seize and maintain campaign information superiority, unify command campaign information operational forces, carry out information warfare-related reconnaissance, and offensive and defensive information warfare methods. According to a PLA military manual, there are many types of supporting IO to campaigns including an island-landing campaign IO, blockade campaign IO, fire power attack campaign IO, border counterattack campaign IO, counter-landing campaign IO, and counter-airstrike campaign IO. These IO campaigns can be sub-divided into joint campaign IO and combined arms campaign IO. Depending on the military services involved in the campaign, IO can be further divided into army campaign, navy, air force, and strategic missile force campaign IO. Their primary tasks are to protect the PLA's campaign information systems, collect intelligence from enemy information systems, destroy enemy information systems, and weaken the enemy's ability to acquire, transmit, process, and use information during war.

The PLA continues to conduct frequent military exercises demonstrating advances in information technology and information integration of its military forces. China has performed integrated joint combat operations exercises showcasing intelligence acquisition, joint command, joint strike, and support operations, increasingly incorporated information technology and information integration into its annual training requirement. A number of annual exercise series, including the *Vanguard*, *Lianhe*, and *Joint Education* series have increased required integration and full reliance on information technology for command of complex operations. In 2012, according to PLA newspapers, many military exercises banned paper maps and orders altogether. Also in 2012, there was an increasing emphasis on PLA command academies participating in joint exercises using command information technologies, which indicates proficiency on such platforms is now a requirement for graduation to higher command positions.

DEVELOPMENTS IN CHINESE MILITARY DOCTRINE AND TRAINING

In 2012, the PLA heavily emphasized training under realistic, high-technology conditions. The Chinese aim to operate in "informatized" conditions by emphasizing system-of-systems operations, a concept similar to U.S. network-centric warfare. This requires linking geographically dispersed forces and capabilities into an integrated system capable of unified action. These operational training reforms are a result of the Outline of Military Training and Evaluation (OMTE), which was last published in mid-2008 and became standard across the PLA on January 1, 2009.

Since that time, the PLA has pushed to achieve OMTE objectives by emphasizing realistic training conditions, training in complex electromagnetic and joint environments, and integrating new and high technologies into the force structure. A result of these changes is a more flexible year-round training cycle, which is a departure from the Soviet-style conscript-dependent training cycles that were prominent throughout the PLA over the previous decades.

Additionally, the PLA is laying the foundation for future changes in military doctrine. To develop a new cadre of officers, the PLA is reforming its academies to cultivate junior officers proficient with and capable of leveraging technology in all warfighting functions for joint operations. The National University of Defense Technology's year-long joint operations staff officer course is serving as a pilot for a future national-level program. The course allows junior officers to rotate to the command elements of other PLA services to enhance their skills in joint operations planning and preparation.

ADVANCED TECHNOLOGY ACQUISITION

China relies on foreign technology, acquisition of key dual-use components, and focused indigenous research and development (R&D) to advance military modernization. The Chinese utilize a large, well-organized network to facilitate collection of sensitive information and export-controlled technology from U.S. defense sources. Many of the organizations composing China's military-industrial complex have both military and civilian research and development functions. This network of government-affiliated companies and research institutes often enables the PLA to access sensitive and dual-use technologies or knowledgeable experts under the guise of civilian research and development. The enterprises and institutes accomplish this through technology conferences and symposia, legitimate contracts and joint commercial ventures, partnerships with foreign firms, and joint development of specific technologies. In the case of key national security technologies, controlled equipment, and other materials not readily obtainable through commercial means or academia, China has utilized its intelligence services and employed other illicit approaches that involve violations of U.S. laws and export controls.

A high-priority for China's advanced technology acquisition strategy is its Civil-Military Integration policy to develop an innovative dual-use technology and industrial base that serve both military and civilian requirements. China's defense industry has benefited from integration with its expanding civilian economy and science and technology sectors, particularly sectors with access to foreign technology. Examples of technologies include: advanced aviation and aerospace (hot section technologies, avionics and flight controls), source code, traveling wave tubes, night vision devices, monolithic microwave integrated circuits, and information and cyber technologies.

Differentiating between civil and military end-use is very challenging in China due to opaque corporate structures, hidden asset ownership, and the connections of commercial personnel with the central government. Some commercial entities are affiliated with PLA research institutes, or have ties to and are subject to the control of government organizations such as the State-owned Assets Supervision and Administration Commission.

In March 2012, Hui Sheng Shen and Huan Ling Chang, both from Taiwan, were charged with conspiracy to violate the U.S. Arms Export Control Act after allegedly intending to acquire and pass sensitive U.S. defense technology to China. The pair planned to photograph the technology, delete the images, bring the memory cards back to China, and have a Chinese contact recover the images.

In June 2012, Pratt & Whitney Canada (PWC), a subsidiary of U.S. aerospace firm and defense contractor United Technologies Corporation (UTC), pleaded guilty to illegally providing military software used in the development of China's Z-10 military attack helicopter.

UTC and two subsidiaries agreed to pay $75 million and were debarred from license privileges as part of a settlement with the U.S. Department of Justice and State Department.

PWC "knowingly and willfully" caused six versions of military electronic engine control software to be "illegally exported" from

Hamilton Sundstrand in the United States to PWC in Canada and then to China for the Z-10, and made false and belated disclosures about these illegal exports.

In September 2012, Sixing Liu, aka "Steve Liu," was convicted of violating the U.S. Arms Export Control Act and the International Traffic in Arms Regulations (ITAR) and possessing stolen trade secrets. Liu, a Chinese citizen, returned to China with electronic files containing details on the performance and design of guidance systems for missiles, rockets, target locators, and unmanned aerial vehicles. Liu developed critical military technology for a U.S. defense contractor and stole the documents to position himself for employment in China.

2

UNDERSTANDING CHINA'S STRATEGY

NATIONAL-LEVEL PRIORITIES AND GOALS

China's leaders characterize the first two decades of the 21ˢᵗ century as a "strategic window of opportunity." They assess that during this period, both domestic and international conditions will be conducive to expanding China's "comprehensive national power," a term that encapsulates all elements of state power, including economic capacity, military might, and diplomacy. China's leaders anticipate that a successful expansion of comprehensive national power will serve China's strategic objectives, which include: perpetuating Chinese Communist Party (CCP) rule, sustaining economic growth and development, maintaining domestic political stability, defending national sovereignty and territorial integrity, and securing China's status as a great power.

China's leaders routinely emphasize the goal of reaching critical economic and military benchmarks by 2020. These benchmarks include successfully restructuring the economy to maintain growth and increase the quality of living of China's citizens to promote stability; making major progress in military modernization; and attaining the capability to fight and win potential regional conflicts, including those related to Taiwan, protection of sea lines of communication (SLOCs), defense of territorial claims in the South China Sea and East China Sea, and the defense of western borders. Statements by Chinese leaders indicate that, in their view, the development of a modern military is necessary for China to achieve greater power status. These statements also indicate that the Chinese leadership views a modern military as a critical deterrent to prevent actions by outside powers that could damage Chinese interests, or to allow China to defend itself against such actions should deterrence fail.

Since China launched its "reform and opening" in late 1978, the essential elements of China's strategy to accomplish these goals have remained relatively constant. Rather than challenge the existing global order, China has adopted a pragmatic approach to international relations and economic development that seeks to strengthen the economy, modernize the military, and solidify the CCP's hold on power. China balances the imperative to reassure countries that its rise is "peaceful" with the imperative to strengthen its control over existing sovereignty and territorial claims.

China regards stable relations with its neighbors and the United States as essential to its stability and development. China continues to see the United States as the dominant regional and global actor with the greatest potential to both support and, potentially, disrupt China's rise. In addition, China remains concerned that should regional states come to view China as a threat, they might balance against China through unilateral military modernization or through coalitions, possibly with the United States. Many Chinese officials and the public see the U.S. rebalance to Asia as a reflection of "Cold War thinking" and as a way to contain China's rise.

Despite its desire to project an image of a developing country engaged in a peaceful development strategy, China's efforts to defend national sovereignty and territorial integrity (underpinned by growing economic and military capabilities) have occasionally manifested in assertive rhetoric and behavior that generate regional concerns about its intentions. Prominent examples of this include China's response to Japan's arrest of a PRC fishing trawler captain following a collision with Japanese coast guard vessels in 2010, its use of punitive trade policies as an instrument of coercion, its actions to shield North Korea from the international response to its sinking of the South Korean naval vessel, *Cheonan*, and its action to pressure Vietnam and the Philippines in the South China Sea and Japan in the East China Sea. Official statements and media during these situations indicate that China sees itself as responding to perceived threats to its national interests or provocations by outside actors. China's lack of transparency surrounding its growing military capabilities and strategic decision-making has also increased concerns in the region about China's intentions. Absent a move towards greater transparency, these concerns will likely intensify as the PLA modernization progresses.

Origin of the "New Historic Missions"

In 2004, former President Hu Jintao articulated a mission statement for the armed forces titled, the "Historic Missions of the Armed Forces in the New Period of the New Century." These "new historic missions" focus primarily on adjustments in the leadership's assessment of the international security environment and the expanding definition of national security. These missions were further codified in a 2007 amendment to the CCP Constitution. The missions, as currently defined, include:

- Provide an important guarantee of strength for the party to consolidate its ruling position.

- Provide a strong security guarantee for safeguarding the period of strategic opportunity for national development.

- Provide a powerful strategic support for safeguarding national interests.

- Play an important role in safeguarding world peace and promoting common development.

According to official writings, the driving factors behind the articulation of these missions were: changes in China's security situation, challenges and priorities regarding China's national development, and a desire to realign the tasks of the PLA with the CCP's objectives. Politburo member and CMC Vice Chairman Xu Caihou in 2005 asserted "the historic missions embody the new requirements imposed on the military by the Party's historic tasks, accommodate new changes in our national development strategy, and conform to the new trends in global military development." While these missions are not expected to replace the defense of China's sovereignty in importance, implications for PLA modernization may be increased preparation for and participation in international peacekeeping and disaster relief operations, interaction with the international community that allows the PLA more opportunities to learn from other militaries, and greater efforts to improve PLA logistics and transport capabilities.

FACTORS SHAPING CHINA'S LEADERSHIP PERCEPTIONS

Chinese leaders continue to view themselves as operating in a "window of opportunity" to advance their priorities of economic development, territorial integrity, and domestic stability. Although domestic stability is believed to be China's top priority, official documents indicate that China sees its security environment becoming more "complex" as a result of several factors:

Economics. Continued economic development remains the bedrock of social stability. A wide range of economic factors could disrupt this trajectory, including a failure to shift away from its overreliance on investment and exports to drive growth. China's leaders scaled back GDP targets for 2011-2015 (from 8 percent to 7.5 percent) to mitigate risk of overheating and to manage expectations. Other potential economic risks for China include shifting global trade patterns, domestic resource constraints, rising wages driven by labor shortages, or attempts to challenge China's access to global resources, including energy.

Nationalism. Communist Party leaders and military officials continue to be affected by, and in some cases exploit, nationalism to bolster the legitimacy of the Party, deflect domestic criticism, and justify their own inflexibility in dialogues with foreign interlocutors. However, nationalist forces could ultimately restrict the leadership's decision-making on key policy issues or pressure the CCP if these forces perceive party leaders as insufficiently satisfying nationalist goals.

Regional Challenges to China's Interests. Tensions with Japan in the East China Sea and with South China Sea claimants challenge to China's desire to maintain a stable periphery. Combined with a greater U.S. presence in the region, these factors raise Chinese concerns that regional countries will strengthen their military capabilities or increase security cooperation with the United States to balance China.

Domestic Unrest. The CCP continues to face long-term popular demands for limiting corruption and improving government responsiveness, transparency, and accountability. If unmet, these factors likely weaken the legitimacy of the CCP in the eyes of the Chinese people. The Arab Spring and fears of a Jasmine Revolution amplify historical concerns about internal stability.

Environment. China's economic development has come at a high environmental cost. China's leaders are increasingly concerned that environmental degradation could undermine regime legitimacy by threatening economic development, public health, social stability, and China's international image.

Demographics. China faces the dual threat of a rapidly aging population and a declining birth rate, one that now falls below replacement level. Longer life expectancies may force China to allocate more resources to social and health services, while the declining birth rate will continue to reduce China's supply of young and inexpensive labor, a key driver of the country's three decades of economic growth. This dual phenomenon could lead to economic stagnation that could threaten CCP legitimacy.

China's Energy Strategy

China's engagement, investment, and foreign construction related to energy continue to grow. China has constructed or invested in energy projects in more than 50 countries, spanning nearly every continent. This ambitious investment in energy assets is driven primarily by two factors. First, China is increasingly dependent upon imported energy to sustain its economy. A net oil exporter until 1993, China remains suspicious of international energy markets. Second, energy projects present a viable option for investing China's vast foreign currency holdings.

In addition to ensuring reliable energy sources, Beijing hopes to diversify producers and transport options. Although energy independence is no longer realistic for China, given population growth and increasing per capita energy consumption, Beijing still seeks to maintain a supply chain that is less susceptible to external disruption.

In 2011, China imported approximately 58 percent of its oil; conservative estimates project that China will import almost two-thirds of its oil by 2015 and three-quarters by 2030. Beijing looks primarily to the Persian Gulf, Africa, and Russia/Central Asia to satisfy its growing demand, with imported oil accounting for approximately 11 percent of China's total energy consumption.

A second goal of Beijing's foreign energy strategy is to alleviate China's heavy dependence on SLOCs, particularly the South China Sea and the Strait of Malacca. In 2011, approximately 85 percent of China's oil imports transited the South China Sea and the Strait of Malacca. Separate crude oil pipelines from Russia and Kazakhstan to China illustrate efforts to increase overland supply. A pipeline that would bypass the Strait of Malacca by transporting crude oil from Kyuakpya, Burma to Kunming, China is currently under construction with an estimated completion time of late 2013 or early 2014. The crude oil for this pipeline will be supplied by Saudi Arabia and other Middle Eastern and African countries.

Given China's growing energy demand, new pipelines will only slightly alleviate China's maritime dependency on either the Strait of Malacca or the Strait of Hormuz. Despite China's efforts, the sheer volume of oil and liquefied natural gas that is imported to China from the Middle East and Africa will make strategic SLOCs increasingly important to Beijing.

In 2011, China imported 14.3 billion cubic meters (bcm) of natural gas, or 46 percent of all of its natural gas imports, from Turkmenistan to China by pipeline via Kazakhstan and Uzbekistan. This pipeline is designed to carry 40 bcm per year with plans to expand it to 60 bcm. Another natural gas pipeline designed to deliver 12 bcm per year of Burmese-produced gas is under construction and estimated for completion in late 2013 or early 2014. This pipeline parallels the crude oil pipeline across Burma. Beijing is negotiating with Moscow for two pipelines that could supply China with up to 69 bcm of gas per year; discussions have stalled over pricing differences.

China's Top Crude Suppliers 2011

Country	Volume (1,000 barrels per day)	Percentage of Imported Crude Oil
Saudi Arabia	1010	20
Angola	626	12
Iran	557	11
Russia	396	8
Oman	365	7
Iraq	277	5
Sudan	261	5
Venezuela	231	5
Kazakhstan	225	4
Kuwait	192	4
Others	956	19
Total	5096	100

INTERNAL DEBATE OVER CHINA'S REGIONAL AND GLOBAL ROLE

China's leadership has supported former paramount leader Deng Xiaoping's dictum from the early 1990s that China should, "observe calmly; secure our position; cope with affairs calmly; hide our capabilities and bide our time; be good at maintaining a low profile; and never claim leadership." This guidance reflected Deng's belief that Chinese interests are best served by focusing on internal development and stability while steering clear of challenging or confronting major powers. In December 2010, State Councilor Dai Bingguo specifically cited Deng's guidance, insisting China adhered to a "path of peaceful development" and would not seek expansion or hegemony. He asserted that the "hide and bide" rhetoric was not a "smokescreen" employed while China builds its strength, but rather an admonition to be patient and not stand out.

However, some Chinese scholars question whether Deng's policy approach will continue to win support as China's interests increase abroad and its power expands. China's perceived security interests have changed considerably since Deng's era to include a heavy reliance on maritime commerce. China's improving naval capabilities enable roles and missions that would have been impossible for the PLA to pursue just a decade ago. Proponents of a more active and assertive Chinese role on the world stage have suggested that China would be better served by a firm stance in the face of U.S. or other regional pressure. These voices could increase as a result of renewed tensions with the Philippines and Vietnam over the South China Sea and with Japan over the Senkakus, further complicating this debate.

"New Type of Relationship." Top Chinese leaders have repeatedly advocated for a "new type of relationship between great powers" in meetings with U.S. officials. The "new type of relationship" concept urges a cooperative U.S.-China partnership based on equality, mutual respect, and mutual benefit. The concept also reflects China's aspirations to be regarded as a great power, emphasizing conflict avoidance to maintain its "peaceful rise."

China's Periphery. The Chinese leadership faces a policy dilemma in seeking to maintain a stable periphery in order to assure its "window of opportunity" for development remains open. China also perceives other regional countries asserting their national interests in China's periphery and feels compelled to respond to ensure continued stability; however, too strong of a response may motivate regional actors to counterbalance China's rise through greater cooperation with each other and the United States. Therefore, China's leaders are trying to maintain a delicate balance between defending territorial integrity in the face of perceived provocations by its neighbors while concurrently tamping down threat perceptions across the globe. China publicly states that its rise is "peaceful" and that it harbors no "hegemonic" designs or aspirations for territorial expansion. However, China's lack of transparency surrounding these growing capabilities has increased concerns in the region about China's intentions.

China's Territorial Disputes

China's use of force in territorial disputes has varied throughout its history. Some disputes led to war, such as China's border conflicts with India in 1962 and Vietnam in 1979. A contested border with the former Soviet Union during the 1960s raised the possibility of nuclear war. In more recent cases, China has been willing to compromise with and even offer concessions to its neighbors. Since 1998, China has settled eleven land-based territorial disputes with six of its neighbors. Several disputes continue over exclusive economic zones (EEZ) and ownership of potentially rich, off-shore oil and gas deposits.

The East China Sea contains approximately seven trillion cubic feet of natural gas and up to 100 billion barrels of oil. Japan maintains that an equidistant line from each country involved should separate the EEZs, while China claims an extended continental shelf beyond the equidistant line to the Okinawa Trench (which almost reaches Japan's shore). In early 2009, Japan accused China of violating a June 2008 agreement providing for joint exploration of oil and natural gas fields, and claimed that China unilaterally drilled beneath the demarcation line, extracting reserves from the Japanese side. China, Japan, and Taiwan continue to dispute possession of the nearby Senkaku Islands.

The South China Sea plays an important role in Northeast and Southeast Asian security considerations. Northeast Asia relies heavily on the flow of oil and commerce through South China Sea shipping lanes, including over 80 percent of the crude oil to Japan, South Korea, and Taiwan. China claims sovereignty over the Spratly and Paracel island groups and other land formations within its "nine-dash line" claim - claims disputed in whole or part by Brunei, the Philippines, Malaysia, Indonesia, and Vietnam. Taiwan, which occupies Itu Aba in the Spratly Islands, makes the same claims as the PRC. In 2009, China protested extended continental shelf claims in the South China Sea made by Malaysia and Vietnam; in its protest to the U.N. Commission, China included the ambiguous nine-dash line and reiterated that it has "indisputable sovereignty over the islands in the South China Sea and the adjacent waters and enjoys sovereign rights and jurisdiction over the relevant waters as well as the seabed and subsoil thereof."

Despite increased political and economic relations over the years between China and India, tensions remain along their shared 4,057 km border, most notably over Arunachal Pradesh (which China asserts is part of Tibet, and therefore of China), and over the Aksai Chin region at the western end of the Tibetan Plateau. Both countries in 2009 stepped up efforts to assert their claims. China tried to block a $2.9 billion loan to India from the Asian Development Bank, claiming part of the loan would have been used for water projects in Arunachal Pradesh. This represented the first time China sought to influence this dispute through a multilateral institution. The then-governor of Arunachal Pradesh announced that India would deploy more troops and fighter jets to the area. An Indian newspaper reported that the number of Chinese border violations had risen from 180 in 2011 to more than 400 by September 2012.

Power Projection Capability. There has also been an active debate among military and civilian theorists in China concerning future capabilities the PLA should develop to advance China's interests beyond traditional requirements. Some senior officers and civilian theorists advocate an expansion of the PLA's power projection capabilities to facilitate missions well beyond Taiwan and regional disputes. Publicly, Chinese officials contend that increasing the scope of China's maritime capabilities is intended to build capacity for international peacekeeping, humanitarian assistance, disaster relief, and protection of sea lanes. The commissioning of the PLA Navy's first aircraft carrier in 2012, in addition to serving as a symbol of national prestige, exemplifies these aspirations.

Indicators of Decision and Intent. There are several possible indicators of change in

Chinese decision-making, depending on the issue. This intent could be reflected through speeches in regional and multi-national organizations, commentary in official, domestic newspapers or prominent Chinese think tanks, adjustments to China's Defense White Paper, changes in talking points with civilian and military interlocutors, disposition of forces, and changes in military diplomacy.

PLA MILITARY ENGAGEMENT

The PLA's level of engagement with foreign militaries continues to grow significantly. At the operational level, this engagement provides the PLA with opportunities to share doctrines, strategies, tactics, techniques, and procedures with other militaries - both modern and developing. At the strategic level, China uses military engagement as a platform for demonstrating the PLA's growing capabilities, its status as a modern military, and its potential role as a responsible security partner.

Senior-level visits and exchanges provide China with opportunities to increase military officers' international exposure, communicate China's positions to foreign audiences, better understand alternative world views, and advance foreign relations through interpersonal contacts and military assistance programs. Expanded PLA travel abroad enables China's military officers to observe and study foreign military command structures, unit formations, and operational training.

The PLA is participating in a growing number of bilateral and multilateral military exercises. The PLA derives political benefit from these exercises in terms of increased influence and enhanced ties with partner states and organizations. These exercises also contribute to PLA modernization by providing opportunities to improve capabilities in areas such as counterterrorism, mobility operations, and logistics. The PLA gains operational insight by observing tactics, command decision making, and equipment used by more advanced militaries.

PLA participation or observer status in military training exercises of nations in possession of U.S. military equipment, systems, and weapons may, in certain circumstances, have unintended consequences that could result in the unauthorized disclosure of defense articles, technical data, or defense services to China. Public Law 101-246 – the Tiananmen Sanctions – prohibits the transfer or disclosure of U.S.-origin defense articles, defense services, technical data, and/or technology to China. Additionally, Public Law 94-329 – the Arms Export Control Act - and the International Traffic in Arms Regulations list China as a nation for which U.S. policy denies the transfer or export of defense articles (including technical data) and defense services.

Beijing primarily conducts arms sales to enhance foreign relationships and to generate revenue to support its domestic defense industry. China's arms sales range from small arms and ammunition to joint development or transfer of advanced weapons systems. Chinese companies sell mostly to developing countries where China's low-cost weapons sales serve a strategic purpose. For example, China maintains strong and longstanding military–technical cooperation with Pakistan, which includes arms sales and defense industrial cooperation. With other countries of strategic importance to China, such as Sudan, arms sales and other security assistance deepen developing ties and balance China's energy imports.

As China's regional and international interests grow more complex, the PLA's international engagement will expand, especially in the areas of peacekeeping operations, counter-piracy, humanitarian assistance/disaster relief (HA/DR), and joint exercises. In addition to furthering PLA modernization, the focus of these engagements will likely remain on building China's political ties, assuaging fears about China's rise, and building China's external influence, particularly in Asia.

China's Military Leadership

The PLA is the armed instrument of the CCP and, organizationally, is subordinate to the Party apparatus. Career military officers are CCP members, and units at the company level and above have political officers responsible for personnel decisions, propaganda, and counterintelligence. Major decisions at all levels are made by CCP committees, also led by the political officers and commanders.

The PLA's highest decision-making body, the Central Military Commission (CMC), is technically a department of the CCP Central Committee, but is staffed primarily by military officers. The CMC Chairman is a civilian, usually the General Secretary of the CCP and President. Other members include several vice chairmen, the commanders of the military services, and the directors of the four general headquarters departments.

China's Ministry of National Defense (MND) is not equivalent to the "defense ministry" in most other nations, but rather is a small office coordinating military-related tasks where responsibility overlaps between the civilian government and the armed forces, including foreign military relations, mobilization, recruitment, "national defense education," and civil support to military operations. The Minister of Defense is a uniformed military officer, a member of the State Council (the country's chief administrative authority), and also a CMC member.

Following the increasing professionalization of the PLA, the military now holds fewer formal positions in key political bodies than in the mid-1990s or even the mid-2000s. With the passing of China's revolutionary generation, few national leaders have served in the military: the Politburo Standing Committee has not had a uniformed member since 1997 and only 4 of the 25 current Politburo members have military experience. However, the PLA remains an influential player in

China's defense and foreign policy due to the CMC's special bureaucratic status and the PLA's near monopoly on military expertise. Even as the PLA remains subordinate to top Party leadership direction as the armed wing of the Chinese Communist Party, longstanding bureaucratic coordination issues and China's increasingly active media landscape have sometimes led to PLA-associated actions or statements that appear to diverge from the positions of China's other key bureaucratic actors, especially on national sovereignty or territorial issues.

Members of the Chinese Communist Party's Central Military Commission (CMC)

Chairman Xi Jinping's appointment as Party General Secretary and CMC chairman, and his expected selection as state president in the spring, represent the first clean transfer of power in recent decades. Prior to becoming China's new commander-in-chief, Xi served as the CMC's only civilian vice chairman. Xi's father was an important military figure during the Chinese communist revolution and a Politburo member in the 1980s. The younger Xi served as secretary to a defense minister early in his career and would have had ample opportunities to interact with the PLA as a provincial Party official. In meetings with U.S. officials Xi has emphasized increasing mutual trust between Beijing and Washington.

Vice Chairman Fan Changlong is Beijing's top uniformed officer. He formerly commanded the Jinan Military Region (MR), a test bed for new operational concepts and technology that has been at the forefront of the PLA's joint training efforts in recent years. Fan was the longest serving of China's seven MR commanders at the time of his promotion to the CMC. He also spent 35 years in the Shenyang MR where he reportedly served in the same unit as outgoing CMC Vice Chairman Xu Caihou, the PLA's top political officer.

Vice Chairman Xu Qiliang—the first career air force officer promoted to CMC vice chairman—previously served on the CMC as PLA Air Force commander where he oversaw rapid force modernization and expanded the air force's foreign engagement. He vocally advocated for increasing the PLA Air Force's role within the larger PLA including arguing in 2009 that the air force should lead the development of offensive space capabilities. Xu may have crossed paths with Xi Jinping earlier in their careers when both men served in Fujian Province. Xu was the first PLA Air Force officer to serve as deputy chief of the General Staff Department (GSD) since the Cultural Revolution period, and—at 54—the youngest in PLA history.

Chang Wanquan was appointed Minister of National Defense at the National People's Congress in March 2013. The Minister of National Defense is the PLA's third most senior officer and manages its relationship with state bureaucracies and foreign militaries. Chang previously oversaw the PLA's weapons development and space portfolio as head of the General Armament Department. He is a veteran of China's border skirmishes with Vietnam and held top posts across military regions.

Chief of the General Staff Department Fang Fenghui oversees PLA operations, training, and intelligence. He served as "commander-in-chief" of China's 60th anniversary military parade in 2009 and oversaw security for the 2008 Beijing Olympic Games. Fan is the first Beijing Military Region commander to move directly to Chief of the General Staff Department. He was the youngest military region commander when he was promoted to lead the Beijing Military Region in 2007.

General Political Department Director Zhang Yang oversees the PLA's political work to include propaganda, discipline, and education. He previously served as Political Commissar of the Guangzhou Military Region, which borders Vietnam and the South China Sea. Zhang assumed that position at a relatively young age and is unusual among the other newly appointed CMC members for spending his entire career in one military region. Zhang also participated in China's border conflict with Vietnam and supported disaster relief efforts following a January 2008 snowstorm in southern China.

General Logistics Department Director Zhao Keshi is responsible for overseeing PLA support functions including finances, land, mining, and construction. Zhao spent his entire career in the Nanjing MR responsible for a Taiwan contingency and most recently served as its Commander. He was also reportedly an exercise commander in the large military drills that induced the 1996 Taiwan Strait Crisis. Zhao has written on defense mobilization and reserve construction.

General Armament Department Director Zhang Youxia is responsible for overseeing the military's weapons development and space program. Nicknamed "General Patton," he has rare experience as a combat commander during China's brief conflict with Vietnam in 1979. Zhang formerly commanded the Shenyang Military Region, which shares a border with North Korea and Russia. Zhang is one of China's military "princelings." His father, a well-known military figure in China, served with Xi Jinping's father in the 1940s.

PLA Navy Commander Wu Shengli has served as head of the navy since 2006 and on the CMC since 2007—only the second PLA Navy Commander to do so in recent decades. Under Wu, the navy has increased its out-of-area exercises, multinational patrols, and foreign naval exchanges, and initiated its first deployment to the Gulf of Aden. The first career navy officer to serve as a Deputy Chief of the General Staff, Wu held leadership positions in two of the PLA Navy's three fleets, spending most of his career in the East Sea Fleet.

PLA Air Force Commander Ma Xiaotian previously oversaw the PLA's military engagement activities as a Deputy Chief of the General Staff. Ma led the PLA side in key military-to-military exchanges with the United States, including the Defense Consultative Talks and the Strategic Security Dialogue component of the U.S.-China Strategic and Economic Dialogue. Ma has significant operational experience both as a pilot and staff officer in multiple military regions.

Second Artillery Commander Wei Fenghe oversees China's strategic missile forces and bases. Wei served in multiple missile bases across different military regions and held top posts in the Second Artillery headquarters before being promoted in late 2010 to Deputy Chief of the General Staff - the first officer from the Second Artillery to do so. In that role, Wei met frequently with foreign delegations, including senior U.S. officials, affording him greater international exposure than previous Second Artillery commanders.

3

FORCE MODERNIZATION GOALS AND TRENDS

OVERVIEW

Although Taiwan continues to dominate the PLA's force modernization agenda (see Chapter Five: Force Modernization for a Taiwan Contingency), Beijing is investing in military programs and weapons designed to improve extended-range power projection and operations in emerging domains such as cyber, space, and electronic warfare. Current trends in China's weapons production will enable the PLA to conduct a range of military operations in Asia well beyond Taiwan, in the South China Sea, western Pacific, and Indian Ocean. Key systems that have been either deployed or are in development include ballistic missiles (including anti-ship variants), anti-ship and land attack cruise missiles, nuclear submarines, modern surface ships, and an aircraft carrier. The need to ensure trade, particularly oil supplies from the Middle East, has prompted China's navy to conduct counter-piracy operations in the Gulf of Aden. Disputes with Japan over maritime claims in the East China Sea and with several Southeast Asian claimants to all or parts of the Spratly and Paracel Islands in the South China Sea have led to renewed tensions in these areas. Instability on the Korean Peninsula could also produce a regional crisis involving China's military. The desire to protect energy investments in Central Asia, along with potential security implications from cross-border support to ethnic separatists, could also provide an incentive for military investment or intervention in this region if instability surfaces.

China's political leaders have also charged the PLA with developing capabilities for missions such as peacekeeping, disaster relief, and counterterrorism operations. These capabilities will increase Beijing's options for military influence to press its diplomatic agenda, advance regional and international interests, and resolve disputes in its favor.

China has become more involved in HA/DR operations in response to the "New Historic Missions." China's ANWEI-class military hospital ship (the *Peace Ark*) has deployed throughout East Asia and to the Caribbean.

China has conducted more than ten joint military exercises with the SCO members, the most prominent being the PEACE MISSION series, with China and Russia as the main participants.

China continues its Gulf of Aden counter-piracy deployment that began in December 2008. Outside of occasional goodwill cruises, this represents the PLA Navy's only series of operational deployments beyond the immediate western Pacific region.

PLA FUTURE CAPABILITIES

Nuclear Weapons. China's official policy on nuclear weapons continues to focus on maintaining a nuclear force structure able to survive an attack and respond with sufficient strength to inflict unacceptable damage on an enemy. The new generation of mobile missiles, with warheads consisting of MIRVs and penetration aids, are intended to ensure the viability of China's strategic deterrent in the face of continued advances in U.S. and, to a lesser extent, Russian strategic intelligence, surveillance, and reconnaissance (ISR), precision strike, and missile defense capabilities. The PLA has deployed new command, control, and communications capabilities to its nuclear forces. These capabilities improve the Second Artillery's ability to command and control multiple units in the field. Through the use of improved communications links, the ICBM units now have better access to battlefield information, uninterrupted communications connecting all command echelons, and the unit commanders are able to issue orders to multiple subordinates at once, instead of serially via voice commands.

China has consistently asserted that it adheres to a "no first use" (NFU) policy, stating it would use nuclear forces only in response to a nuclear strike against China. China's NFU pledge consists of two stated commitments:

China will never use nuclear weapons first against any nuclear-weapon state, and China will never use or threaten to use nuclear weapons against any non-nuclear-weapon state or nuclear-weapon-free zone. However, there is some ambiguity over the conditions under which China's NFU policy would apply, including whether strikes on what China considers its own territory, demonstration strikes, or high-altitude bursts would constitute a first use. Moreover, some PLA officers have written publicly of the need to spell out conditions under which China might need to use nuclear weapons first; for example, if an enemy's conventional attack threatened the survival of China's nuclear force or of the regime itself. However, there has been no indication that national leaders are willing to attach such nuances and caveats to China's NFU doctrine.

China will likely continue to invest considerable resources to maintain a limited, but survivable, nuclear force (sometimes described as "sufficient and effective"), to ensure the PLA can deliver a damaging retaliatory nuclear strike.

Land-Based Platforms. China's nuclear arsenal currently consists of approximately 50-75 ICBMs, including the silo-based CSS-4 (DF-5); the solid-fueled, road-mobile CSS-10 Mods 1 and 2 (DF-31 and DF-31A); and the more limited range CSS-3 (DF-4). This force is complemented by liquid-fueled CSS-2 intermediate-range ballistic missiles and road-mobile, solid-fueled CSS-5 (DF-21) MRBMs for regional deterrence missions. By 2015, China's nuclear forces will include additional CSS-10 Mod 2 and enhanced CSS-4 ICBMs.

Sea-Based Platforms. China continues to produce the JIN-class SSBN, with three already delivered and as many as two more in various stages of construction. The JIN-class SSBNs will eventually carry the JL-2 submarine-launched ballistic missile with an estimated range of 7,400 km. The JIN-class and the JL-2 will give the PLA Navy its first long-range, sea-based nuclear capability. After a round of successful testing in 2012, the JL-2 appears ready to reach initial operational capability in 2013. JIN-class SSBNs based at Hainan Island in the South China Sea would then be able to conduct nuclear deterrence patrols.

Future Efforts. China is working on a range of technologies to attempt to counter U.S. and other countries' ballistic missile defense systems, including maneuverable reentry vehicles (MaRVs), MIRVs, decoys, chaff, jamming, thermal shielding, and anti-satellite (ASAT) weapons. China's official media also cite numerous Second Artillery training exercises featuring maneuver, camouflage, and launch operations under simulated combat conditions, which are intended to increase survivability. Together with the increased mobility and survivability of the new generation of missiles, these technologies and training enhancements strengthen China's nuclear force and enhance its strategic strike capabilities. Further increases in the number of mobile ICBMs and the beginning of SSBN deterrence patrols will force the PLA to implement more sophisticated command and control systems and processes that safeguard the integrity of nuclear release authority for a larger, more dispersed force.

Anti-Access/Area Denial (A2/AD). As part of its planning for military contingencies, China continues to develop measures to deter or counter third-party intervention, particularly by the United States. China's approach to dealing with this challenge is manifested in a sustained effort to develop the capability to attack, at long ranges, military forces that might deploy or operate within the western Pacific, which the DoD characterizes as "anti-access" and "area denial" (A2/AD) capabilities. China is pursuing a variety of air, sea, undersea, space and counter-space, and information warfare systems and operational concepts to achieve this capability, moving toward an array of overlapping, multilayered offensive capabilities extending from China's coast into the western Pacific. China's 2008 Defense White Paper asserts, for example, that one of the priorities for the development of China's armed forces is to "increase the country's capabilities to maintain maritime, space, and electromagnetic space security."

An essential element, if not a fundamental prerequisite, of China's emerging A2/AD regime is the ability to control and dominate the information spectrum in all dimensions of the modern battlespace. PLA authors often cite the need in modern warfare to control information, sometimes termed "information blockade" or "information dominance," and to seize the initiative and gain an information advantage in the early phases of a campaign to achieve air and sea superiority. China is improving information and operational security to protect its own information structures, and is also developing electronic and information warfare capabilities, including denial and deception, to defeat those of its adversaries. China's "information blockade" likely envisions employment of military and non-military instruments of state power across the battlespace, including in cyberspace and outer space. China's investments in advanced electronic warfare systems, counter-space weapons, and computer network operations (CNO) — combined with more traditional forms of control historically associated with the PLA and CCP systems, such as propaganda and denial through opacity, reflect the emphasis and priority China's leaders place on building capability for information advantage.

In more traditional domains, China's A2/AD focus appears oriented toward restricting or controlling access to China's periphery, including the western Pacific. China's current and projected force structure improvements, for example, will provide the PLA with systems that can engage adversary surface ships up to 1,000 nm from China's coast.

China is also developing weapons for its entire military to project force further from its coast.

Current and projected missile systems will allow the PLA to strike regional air bases, logistical facilities, and other ground-based infrastructure. Chinese military analysts have concluded that logistics and power projection are potential vulnerabilities in modern warfare, given the requirements for precision in coordinating transportation, communications, and logistics networks. China is fielding an array of conventionally armed ballistic missiles, ground- and air-launched land-attack cruise missiles, special operations forces, and cyber-warfare capabilities to hold targets at risk throughout the region.

Counter-Space. PLA strategists regard the ability to utilize space and deny adversaries access to space as central to enabling modern, informatized warfare. Although PLA doctrine does not appear to address space operations as a unique operational "campaign," space operations form an integral component of other PLA campaigns and would serve a key role in enabling A2/AD operations. Publicly, China attempts to dispel any skepticism over its military intentions for space. In 2009, PLA Air Force Commander General Xu Qiliang publically retracted his earlier assertion that the militarization of space was a "historic inevitability" after President Hu Jintao swiftly contradicted him. General Xu Qiliang is now a Vice Chairman of the Central Military Commission and the second highest-ranking officer in the PLA.

The PLA is acquiring a range of technologies to improve China's space and counter-space capabilities. China demonstrated a direct-ascent kinetic kill anti-satellite capability to low Earth orbit when it destroyed the defunct Chinese FY-1C weather satellite during a test in January 2007. Although Chinese defense academics often publish on counterspace threat technologies, no additional anti-satellite programs have been publicly acknowledged. A PLA analysis of U.S. and coalition military operations reinforced the importance of operations in space to enable "informatized" warfare, claiming that "space is the commanding point for the information battlefield." PLA writings emphasize the necessity of "destroying, damaging, and interfering with the enemy's reconnaissance...and communications satellites," suggesting that such systems, as well as navigation and early warning satellites, could be among the targets of attacks designed to "blind and deafen the enemy." The same PLA analysis of U.S. and coalition military operations also states that "destroying or capturing satellites and other sensors…will deprive an opponent of initiative on the battlefield and [make it difficult] for them to bring their precision guided weapons into full play."

Information Operations. New technologies allow the PLA to share intelligence, battlefield information, logistics information, weather reports, etc., instantaneously (over robust and redundant communications networks), resulting in improved situational awareness for commanders. In particular, by enabling the sharing of near-real-time ISR data with commanders in the field, decision-making processes are facilitated, shortening command timelines and making operations more efficient.

These improvements have greatly enhanced the PLA's flexibility and responsiveness. "Informatized" operations no longer require meetings for command decision-making or labor-intensive processes for execution. Commanders can now issue orders to multiple units at the same time while on the move, and units can rapidly adjust their actions through the use of digital databases and command automation tools. This is critical for joint operations needed to execute A2/AD. However, to fully implement "informatized" command and control, the PLA will need to overcome a shortage of trained personnel and its culture of centralized, micro-managed command.

The PLA GSD Fourth Department (Electronic Countermeasures and Radar) would likely use information operations (IO) tools, to include jamming/EW, CNO, and deception to augment counter-space and other kinetic operations during a wartime scenario. "Simultaneous and parallel" operations would involve strikes against U.S. warships, aircraft, and associated supply craft and the use of IO to affect tactical and operational communications and computer networks. The PLA would likely rely on IO to disrupt the U.S. capability to use navigational and targeting radar.

Maritime. The PLA Navy is in the forefront of China's A2/AD developments, having the greatest range and staying power within the PLA to interdict third-party forces. In a near-term conflict, PLA Navy operations would likely begin in the offshore and coastal areas with attacks by coastal defense cruise missiles, maritime strike aircraft, and smaller combatants, and extend as far as the second island chain and Strait of Malacca using large surface ships and submarines. As the PLA Navy gains experience and acquires larger numbers of more capable platforms, including those with long-range air defense, it will expand the depth of these operations further into the Western Pacific. It will also develop a new capability for ship-based land-attack using cruise missiles. China views long-range anti-ship cruise missiles as a key weapon in this type of operation and is developing multiple advanced types and the platforms to employ them for this purpose. These platforms include conventional and nuclear-powered attack submarines (KILO SS, SONG SS, YUAN SSP, SHANG SSN), surface combatants (LUYANG III DDG [Type 052D], LUZHOU DDG [Type 051C], LUYANG I/II DDG [Type 052B/C], SOVREMENNY II-class DDG, JIANGKAI II FFG [Type 054A], JIANGDAO FFL [Type 056]), and maritime strike aircraft (JH-7 and JH-7A, H-6G, and the SU-30 MK2).

China would face several short-comings in a near-term A2/AD operation. First, it has not developed a robust, deep water anti-submarine warfare capability, in contrast to its strong capabilities in the air and surface domains. Second, it is not clear whether China has the capability to collect accurate targeting information and pass it to launch platforms in time for successful strikes in sea areas beyond the first island chain. However, China is working to overcome these shortcomings.

Air and Air Defense. China's future air force A2/AD capabilities will be bolstered by the development of a 5th generation fighter force, which is not likely to be fielded before 2018. Key characteristics of fifth generation fighters include high maneuverability, lack of visibility on radar due to very low observable stealth shaping, and an internal weapons bay. Other key features of these aircraft are modern avionics and sensors that offer more timely situational awareness for operations in network-centric combat environments, radars with advanced targeting capabilities and protection against enemy electronic countermeasures, and integrated electronic warfare systems with advanced communication and GPS navigation functions. These next generation aircraft will improve China's existing fleet of fourth generation aircraft (Russian built Su-27/Su-30 and indigenous J-10 and J-11B fighters) by utilizing low-observable platforms to support regional air superiority and strike operations. Additionally, China's continuing upgrades to its bomber fleet may provide the capability to carry new, longer-range cruise missiles. Similarly, the acquisition and development of longer-range unmanned aerial vehicles (UAV), including the BZK-005, and unmanned combat aerial vehicles (UCAV), will increase China's ability to conduct long-range reconnaissance and strike operations.

China's ground-based air defense A2/AD capabilities will likely be focused on countering long-range airborne strike platforms with increasing numbers of advanced, long-range SAMs. China's current air and air defense A2/AD components include a combination of advanced long-range SAMs – its indigenous HQ-9 and Russian SA-10 and SA-20 PMU1/PMU2, which have the advertised capability to protect against both aircraft and low-flying cruise missiles. China continues to pursue the acquisition of the Russian extremely long-range S-400 SAM system (400 km), and is also expected to continue research and development to extend the range of the domestic HQ-9 SAM to beyond 200km.

Ballistic Missile Defense. China has made efforts to go beyond defense from aircraft and cruise missiles to gain a ballistic missile defense capability in order to provide further protection of China's mainland and strategic assets. China's existing long-range SAM inventory offers limited capability against ballistic missiles. The SA-20 PMU2, the most advanced SAM Russia offers for export, has the advertised capability to engage ballistic missiles with ranges of 1,000km and speeds of 2,800m/s. China's domestic CSA-9 long-range SAM system is expected to have a limited capability to provide point defense against tactical ballistic missiles with ranges up to 500km. China is proceeding with the research and development of a missile defense umbrella consisting of kinetic energy intercept at exo-atmospheric altitudes (>80km), as well as intercepts of ballistic missiles and other aerospace vehicles within the upper atmosphere. In January 2010, and again in January 2013, China successfully intercepted a ballistic missile at mid-course, using a ground-based missile.

Cyber Activities Directed Against the Department of Defense. In 2012, numerous computer systems around the world, including those owned by the U.S. government, continued to be targeted for intrusions, some of which appear to be attributable directly to the Chinese government and military. These intrusions were focused on exfiltrating information. China is using its computer network exploitation (CNE) capability to support intelligence collection against the U.S. diplomatic, economic, and defense industrial base sectors that support U.S. national defense programs. The information targeted could potentially be used to benefit China's defense industry, high technology industries, policymaker interest in US leadership thinking on key China issues, and military planners building a picture of U.S. network defense networks, logistics, and related military capabilities that could be exploited during a crisis. Although this alone is a serious concern, the accesses and skills required for these intrusions are similar to those necessary to conduct computer network attacks. China's 2010 Defense White Paper notes China's own concern over foreign cyberwarfare efforts and highlighted the importance of cyber-security in China's national defense.

Cyberwarfare in China's Military. Cyberwarfare capabilities could serve Chinese military operations in three key areas. First and foremost, they allow data collection for intelligence and computer network attack purposes. Second, they can be employed to constrain an adversary's actions or slow response time by targeting network-based logistics, communications, and commercial activities. Third, they can serve as a force multiplier when coupled with kinetic attacks during times of crisis or conflict.

Developing cyber capabilities for warfare is consistent with authoritative PLA military writings. Two military doctrinal writings, *Science of Strategy,* and *Science of Campaigns* identify information warfare (IW) as integral to achieving information superiority and an effective means for countering a stronger foe. Although neither document identifies the specific criteria for employing computer network attack against an adversary, both advocate developing capabilities to compete in this medium.

The *Science of Strategy* and *Science of Campaigns* detail the effectiveness of IW and CNO in conflicts and advocate targeting adversary C2 and logistics networks to affect their ability to operate during the early stages of conflict. As *Science of Strategy* explains, "In the information war, the command and control system is the heart of information collection, control, and application on the battlefield. It is also the nerve center of the entire battlefield."

In parallel with its military preparations, China has increased diplomatic engagement and advocacy in multilateral and international forums where cyber issues are discussed and debated. Beijing's agenda is frequently in line with Russia's efforts to promote more international control over cyber activities. China and Russia continue to promote an Information Security Code of Conduct that would have governments exercise sovereign authority over the flow of information and control of content in cyberspace. Both governments also continue to play a disruptive role in multilateral efforts to establish transparency and confidence-building measures in international fora such as the Organization for Security and Cooperation in Europe (OSCE), ASEAN Regional Forum, and the UN Group of Governmental Experts. Although China has not yet agreed with the U.S. position that existing mechanisms, such as international humanitarian law, apply in cyberspace, Beijing's thinking continues to evolve.

Role of Electronic Warfare (EW) in Future Conflict

An integral component of warfare, the PLA identifies EW as a way to reduce or eliminate U.S. technological advantages. Chinese EW doctrine emphasizes using electromagnetic spectrum weapons to suppress or deceive enemy electronic equipment. PLA EW strategy focuses on radio, radar, optical, infrared, and microwave frequencies, in addition to adversarial computer and information systems.

Chinese EW strategy stresses that it is a vital fourth dimension to combat and should be considered equally with traditional ground, sea, and air forces. Effective EW is seen as a decisive aid during military operations and consequently the key to determining the outcome of war. The Chinese see EW as an important force multiplier and would likely employ it in support of all combat arms and services during a conflict.

PLA EW units have conducted jamming and anti-jamming operations testing the military's understanding of EW weapons, equipment, and performance, which helped improve their confidence in conducting force-on-force, real-equipment confrontation operations in simulated electronic warfare environments. The advances in research and deployment of electronic warfare weapons are being tested in these exercises and have proven effective. These EW weapons include jamming equipment against multiple communication and radar systems and GPS satellite systems. EW systems are also being deployed with other sea and air-based platforms intended for both offensive and defensive operations.

Systems and Capabilities Enabling Power Projection. China has prioritized land-based ballistic and cruise missile programs to extend its strike warfare capabilities further from its borders. It is developing and testing several new classes and variants of offensive missiles, forming additional missile units, upgrading older missile systems, and developing methods to counter ballistic missile defenses. The Second Artillery has deployed more than 1,100 SRBMs to garrisons across from Taiwan and is fielding cruise missiles, including the ground-launched CJ-10 land-attack cruise missile. China continues to field an ASBM based on a variant of the DF-21 (CSS-5) medium-range ballistic missile that it began deploying in 2010. Known as the DF-21D, this missile provides the PLA the capability to attack large ships, including aircraft carriers, in the western Pacific. The DF-21D has a range exceeding 1,500 km and is armed with a maneuverable warhead.

The PLA Navy continues the development and deployment of ship, submarine, and aircraft-deployed ASCMs, Russian- and Chinese-built. New long-range air-launched cruise missiles for the H-6 bomber fleet extend the PLA's strike range.

The PLA Air Force is continuing a modernization effort to improve its capability to conduct offensive and defensive off-shore operations such as strike, air and missile defense, strategic mobility, and early warning and reconnaissance missions. China continues its development of stealth aircraft technology, with the appearance of a second stealth fighter following on the heels of the maiden flight of the J-20 in January 2011. In an effort to address its strategic airlift deficiency, as mentioned earlier in this report, China is also developing a heavy lift transport aircraft, possibly identified as the Y-20.

Capabilities to Realize a "Blue Water" Navy. The PLA Navy remains at the forefront of the military's efforts to extend its operational reach beyond East Asia and into what China calls the "far seas." Missions in these areas include protecting important sea lanes from terrorism, maritime piracy, and foreign interdiction; providing humanitarian assistance and disaster relief; conducting naval diplomacy and regional deterrence; and training to prevent a third party, such as the United States, from interfering with operations off China's coast in a Taiwan or South China Sea conflict. The PLA Navy's ability to perform these missions is modest but growing as it gains more experience operating in distant waters and acquires larger and more advanced platforms. The PLA Navy's goal over the coming decades is to become a stronger regional force that is able to project power across the globe for high-intensity operations over a period of several months, similar to the United Kingdom's deployment to the South Atlantic to retake the Falkland Islands in the early 1980s. However, logistics and intelligence support remain key obstacles, particularly in the Indian Ocean.

In the last several years, the PLA Navy's distant seas experience has primarily derived from its ongoing counter-piracy mission in the Gulf of Aden and long-distance task group deployments beyond the first island chain in the western Pacific. China continues to sustain a three-ship presence in the Gulf of Aden to protect Chinese merchant shipping from maritime piracy. This operation is China's first enduring naval operation beyond the Asia region.

Additionally, the PLA Navy has begun to conduct military activities within the Exclusive Economic Zones (EEZs) of other nations, without the permission of those coastal states. Of note, the United States has observed over the past year several instances of Chinese naval activities in the EEZ around Guam and Hawaii. One of those instances was during the execution of the annual Rim of the Pacific (RIMPAC) exercise in July/August 2012. While the United States considers the PLA Navy activities in its EEZ to be lawful, the activity undercuts China's decades-old position that similar foreign military activities in China's EEZ are unlawful.

The PLA Navy has made long-distance deployments a routine part of the annual training cycle. In 2012, it deployed task groups beyond the first island chain seven times with formations as large as seven ships. These deployments are designed to complete a number of training requirements, including long-distance navigation, C2, and multi-discipline warfare in deep sea environments beyond the range of land-based air defense.

The PLA Navy's force structure continues to evolve, incorporating more platforms with the versatility for both offshore and long-distance operations. In addition to the recently-commissioned KUZNETSOV-class aircraft carrier (CV) *Liaoning*, China is engaged in series production of the LUYANG-class III DDG, the JIANGKAI-class II FFG, and the JIANGDAO-class FFL. China will also begin construction on a new Type 081-class landing helicopter assault ship within the next five years. China will probably build several aircraft carriers over the next 15 years.

Limited logistical support remains a key obstacle preventing the PLA Navy from operating more extensively beyond East Asia, particularly in the Indian Ocean. China desires to expand its access to logistics in the Indian Ocean and will likely establish several access points in this area in the next 10 years (potential sites include the Strait of Malacca, Lomboc Strait, and Sunda Strait). These arrangements will likely take the form of agreements for refueling, replenishment, crew rest, and low-level maintenance. The services provided will likely fall short of U.S.-style agreements permitting the full spectrum of support from repair to re-armament.

China's Maritime Security Approach

During the 2012 Scarborough Reef and Senkaku Island tensions, the China Maritime Surveillance (CMS) and Fisheries Law Enforcement Command (FLEC) ships were responsible for directly managing the disputes on a daily basis, while the PLA Navy maintained a more distant presence away from the immediate vicinity of the contested waters. China prefers to use its civilian maritime agencies in these disputes, and use the PLA Navy further ashore from disputed areas or as an escalatory measure. The five civilian agency entities, commonly referred to as the "Five Dragons" are:

Anti-Smuggling Bureau (ASB): Subordinate to the General Administration of Customs and Ministry of Public Security. Armed entity responsible for criminal investigations and smuggling cases along China's inland border posts and rivers.

China Coast Guard (CCG): Subordinate to the Ministry of Public Security. Active duty maritime police force responsible for combating maritime crime.

China Maritime Surveillance (CMS): Subordinate to the State Oceanic Administration and Ministry of Land and Resources. Responsible for asserting China's marine rights and sovereignty claims in disputed maritime regions.

Fisheries Law Enforcement Command (FLEC): Subordinate to the Ministry of Agriculture. Enforces PRC fisheries laws and handles fishery disputes with foreign entities across China's exclusive economic zone (EEZ).

Maritime Safety Administration (MSA): Subordinate to the Ministry of Transport. Responsible for safety of life at sea (SOLAS), maritime pollution control, and cleanup, port inspection, and maritime investigation.

In the next decade, an expanded and modernized force of civilian maritime ships will afford China the capability to more robustly patrol its territorial claims in the ECS and SCS. China is continuing with the second half of a modernization and construction program for its maritime law enforcement agencies. The first half of this program, from 2004-2008, resulted in the addition of almost 20 ocean-going patrol ships for the CMS (9), Bureau of Fisheries (BOF) (3), Maritime Safety Administration (MSA) (3), and China Coast Guard (2). The second half of this program, from 2011-2015, includes at least 30 new ships for the CMS (23), BOF (6), and MSA (1). Several agencies have also acquired ships that were decommissioned from the PLA Navy. Some old patrol ships will be decommissioned during this period. In addition, MLE agencies will likely build more than 100 new patrol craft and smaller units, both to increase capability and to replace old units. Overall, CMS total force level is expected to increase 50 percent by 2020 and BOF by 25 percent. MSA, China Coast Guard, and Maritime Customs force levels will probably remain constant, but with larger and more capable units replacing older, smaller units. Some of these ships will have the capability to embark helicopters, a capability that only a few MLE ships currently have. The enlargement and modernization of China's MLE forces will improve China's ability to enforce its maritime sovereignty.

Military Operations Other Than War.
China's military continues to emphasize Military Operations Other Than War (MOOTW) including emergency response, counter-terrorism, international rescue, disaster relief, peacekeeping, and various other security tasks. China's 2010 Defense White Paper cited the use of its military for these purposes as a means of maintaining social harmony and stability. These missions support the "New Historic Missions" while enabling the PLA opportunities to acquire operational and mobilization proficiency in addition to strengthening civil-military relations.

According to Chinese media, between 2008 and 2011, the PLA employed more than 2.4 million active-duty forces, roughly 7.82 million militia and reservists, and more than 6,700 aircraft sorties for MOOTW, including high-profile events such as the 2008 Beijing Olympics and the 2011 evacuation of Chinese citizens from Libya. Within the past year, China's MOOTW experience has included dispatching soldiers to work with civilian entities to provide disaster relief in Yunnan Province following a 5.6 magnitude earthquake in September, and counter-piracy patrols in the Gulf of Aden. Additionally, the PLA has increasingly committed itself to UN peacekeeping operations and continues military engagements as a member of the SCO.

In December 2011, the Military Operations Other Than War Research Center was founded at the Academy of Military Sciences in Beijing, indicating MOOTW's growing role in the PLA following the establishment of guidelines and regulations for such operations during the preceding two years. This increased emphasis of MOOTW provides the PLA experience with joint operations and various command and control scenarios. Depending on the nature of the operation, PLA resources for MOOTW can be under the command of local jurisdiction or up to the highest levels of civilian and military leadership, allowing the PLA to rapidly respond to unexpected events.

Precision Strike

Short-Range Ballistic Missiles (< 1,000 km): The Second Artillery had more than 1,100 SRBMs at the end of 2012, a modest increase over the past year. The Second Artillery continues to field advanced variants with improved ranges and more sophisticated payloads, while gradually replacing earlier generations that do not possess true precision strike capability.

Medium-Range Ballistic Missiles (1,000-3,000 km): The PLA is fielding conventional MRBMs to increase the range at which it can conduct precision strikes against land targets and naval ships (including aircraft carriers) operating far from China's shores out to the first island chain.

Intermediate-Range Ballistic Missiles (3,000-5,000 km): The PLA is developing conventional intermediate-range ballistic missiles (IRBM), increasing its capability for near-precision strike out to the second island chain. The PLA Navy is also improving its over-the-horizon (OTH) targeting capability with sky wave and surface wave OTH radars, which can be used in conjunction with reconnaissance satellites to locate targets at great distances from China (thereby supporting long-range precision strikes, including employment of ASBMs).

Land-Attack Cruise Missiles: The PLA continues to field air- and ground-launched LACMs for stand-off, precision strikes. Air-launched cruise missiles include the YJ-63, KD-88, and the CJ-20.

Ground Attack Munitions: The PLA Air Force has a small number of tactical air-to-surface missiles as well as precision-guided munitions including all-weather, satellite-guided bombs, anti-radiation missiles, and laser-guided bombs.

Anti-Ship Cruise Missiles: The PLA Navy is deploying the domestically-produced, ship-launched YJ-62 ASCM; the Russian SS-N-22/SUNBURN supersonic ASCM, which is fitted on China's SOVREMENNY-class DDGs acquired from Russia; and the Russian SS-N-27B/SIZZLER supersonic ASCM on China's Russian-built KILO SS. It has, or is acquiring, nearly a dozen ASCM variants, ranging from the 1950s-era CSS-N-2 to the modern Russian-made SS-N-22 and SS-N-27B. China is working to develop a domestically-built supersonic cruise missile capability. The pace of ASCM research, development, and production has accelerated over the past decade.

Anti-Radiation Weapons: China is starting to integrate an indigenous version of the Russian Kh-31P (AS-17) known as the YJ-91 into its fighter-bomber force. The PLA imported Israeli-made HARPY UAVs and Russian-made anti-radiation missiles during the 1990s.

Artillery-Delivered High Precision Munitions: The PLA is developing or deploying artillery systems with the range to strike targets within or even across the Taiwan Strait, including the PHL-03 300 mm multiple-rocket launcher (MRL) (100+ km range) and the longer-range AR-3 dual-caliber MRL (out to 220 km).

Second Artillery: As detailed elsewhere in this report, the Second Artillery is expanding its conventional MRBM force and developing IRBMs to extend the distance from which it can threaten other countries with conventional precision or near-precision strikes.

China's Internal Security Forces

China's internal security forces primarily consist of the People's Armed Police (PAP), the Ministry of Public Security (MPS), and the PLA. The PAP is a paramilitary organization whose primary mission is domestic security. It falls under the dual command of the CMC and the State Council. Although there are different types of PAP units, such as border security and firefighting, the largest is internal security. PAP units are organized into "contingents" in each province, autonomous region, and centrally administered city. In addition, 14 PLA divisions were transferred to the PAP in the mid- to late-1990s to form "mobile divisions" that can deploy outside their home province. The official budget for China's internal security forces exceeds that of the PLA.

The key mission of the MPS is domestic law enforcement and the "maintenance of social security and order," with duties including anti-riot and anti-terrorism. There are approximately 1.9 million MPS police officers spread throughout local public security bureaus across the country.

The PLA's main mission is external security, but assumes internal stability missions when needed. For example, the PLA may provide transportation, logistics, and intelligence. China may also task the militia to assist local public security forces with internal security roles, including protection of infrastructure and maintaining public order.

Chinese leaders perceive threats to the country's internal security coming from popular protests regarding social, economic, environmental, and political problems. Beijing also perceives a security challenge from external non-state actors, such as the separatist East Turkestan Independence Movement and its reported connection with ethnic Uighur nationalist movements in the Xinjiang region.

China activated security forces, but not the PLA, in 2012 to quell incidents ranging from anti-foreign sentiment to socio-economic protests. China deployed paramilitary police in September to control anti-Japanese protesters across multiple cities during the Senkaku Islands dispute. Also in September, paramilitary police mobilized to a Foxconn Manufacturing factory in Shanxi province to put down a riot involving poor pay and working conditions. MPS forces and paramilitary police have deployed multiple times in 2012 to Sichuan and Qinghai provinces to control unrest over self-immolations of monks protesting Chinese rule over Tibet.

4

RESOURCES FOR FORCE MODERNIZATION

OVERVIEW

The PLA continues to decrease its reliance on foreign weapons acquisitions in more capability areas as China's defense-industrial and research bases mature. However, the PLA still looks to foreign assistance to fill some critical near-term capability gaps. China continues to leverage foreign investments, commercial joint ventures, academic exchanges, the experience of repatriated Chinese students and researchers, and state-sponsored industrial and technical espionage to increase the level of technologies and expertise available to support military research, development, and acquisition. Beijing's long-term goal is to create a wholly-indigenous defense industrial sector, augmented by a strong commercial sector, to meet the needs of PLA modernization and to compete as a top-tier producer in the global arms market. China draws from diverse sources to support PLA modernization, including: domestic defense investments, indigenous defense industrial development, a growing research and development/science and technology base, dual-use technologies, and foreign technology acquisition.

MILITARY EXPENDITURES TRENDS

On March 5, 2013, Beijing announced a 10.7 percent increase in its annual military budget to $114 billion, continuing more than two decades of sustained annual defense spending increases. Analysis of data from 2003 through 2012 indicates China's officially disclosed military budget grew at an average of 9.7 percent per year in inflation-adjusted terms over the period. China has the fiscal strength and political will to support defense spending growth at comparable levels, despite lowering its economic growth forecast in 2012 to 7.5 percent from 8 percent in 2011. Continued increases will support PLA modernization efforts and facilitate China's move toward a more professional force.

Estimating China's Actual Military Expenditures. Using 2012 prices and exchange rates, the DoD estimates that China's total actual military-related expenditure for 2012 falls between $135 billion and $215 billion.

However, it is difficult to estimate actual PLA military expenses due to China's poor accounting transparency and incomplete transition from a command economy. China's published military budget omits several major categories of expenditure, such as procurement of foreign weapons and equipment.

2012 Defense Budget Comparison (Adjusted for Inflation)	
	Billion (USD)
China (Official Budget)	$106.7
Russia (National Defense Budget)	$61.3
Japan	$58.0
India	$45.5
Republic of Korea	$29.2
Taiwan	$10.8

Comparison of China's official defense budgets with those of other regional powers.

DEVELOPMENTS AND TRENDS IN CHINA'S DEFENSE INDUSTRY

Defense Sector Reform. China's defense industry has undergone a dramatic transformation since the late 1990s and its companies and research institutes continue to re-organize in an effort to improve weapon system research, development, and production capabilities. China also continues to improve business practices, streamline bureaucracy, shorten developmental timelines, and improve quality control.

In 1998, China adopted a comprehensive strategy for improving defense industrial capabilities. This strategy called for selective modernization in key capabilities areas, increased civil-military industrial integration to leverage available dual use technologies, and the acquisition of advanced foreign weapons, materiel and technologies. An overarching goal of these reforms was to introduce the "Four Mechanisms" of competition, evaluation, supervision, and encouragement into the entire defense industrial system. In 1999, the State Council implemented structural reforms within defense industries to increase competition and efficiency and to make China's defense industry more responsive to the PLA's operational requirements. Each of China's five state-owned defense conglomerates was split into two enterprises, creating a parallel structure in which each would produce both defense and civilian products, encouraging the potential for competition. The production of civilian-use commercial products allows legitimate access to the latest industry and dual-use technologies, which can then be used to support military production. Commercial operations also provide revenue streams to support defense-related activities.

In 2003, the Sixteenth Party Congress introduced the concept of locating military potential in civilian capabilities. It calls for building a civilian industrial sector capable of meeting the needs of military force modernization. In a further move to strengthen the defense sector and improve oversight, China created a new super ministry in 2008. The Ministry of Industry and Informatization (MIIT) was charged with facilitating civil-military integration and the coordinated development of advanced technology and industry. Other structural reforms were adopted to strengthen defense research, development, and production and to bring them more in line with market principles.

China is also emphasizing integration of defense and civilian sectors to leverage output from China's expanding science and technology base. Select defense firms operate research institutes with academic departments, some of which are capable of granting advanced degrees. These institutes serve to focus scientific research on cutting-edge military technologies and to groom the next generation of scientists and engineers who will support defense research, development, and production. These institutes also provide an access point to international resources and

scientific research networks. Chinese practitioners and students at these defense institutes regularly attend conferences, present research findings, and publish scholarly articles.

The China Academy of Sciences (CAS) also plays a key role in facilitating research that supports advancements in military modernization. The CAS Institute of Mechanics is one example, with a mission focus on scientific innovation and high tech integration in aerospace technology, environmental engineering, and energy resources. Specific areas of emphasis include nano-scale and micro-scale mechanics, high temperature gas and supersonic flight technologies, and advanced manufacturing. In May 2012, the Institute announced successful acceptance testing of its new super-large JF12 hypersonic wind tunnel (reportedly the largest in the world), capable of replicating flying conditions at mach 5 to 9. This project was one of eight detailed in China's National Mid-and-Long-Term Scientific and Technological Development Outline Plan (2006-2020). This facility and others like it sponsored by CAS will support research and development efforts in China's civilian and military aerospace sector.

Military Equipment Modernization Trends. China's defense industry resource and investment prioritization and allocation favors missile and space systems, followed by maritime assets and aircraft, and, lastly, ground force materiel. China is developing and producing increasingly advanced systems, augmented through selected investments into foreign designs and reverse engineering. However, China's defense industries are increasing the quality of output in all of these areas as well as increasing overall production capacities. Over the past decade, China has made dramatic improvements in all defense industrial production sectors and is comparable to other major weapon system producers like Russia and the European Union in some areas.

Missile and Space Industry. China's production of a range of ballistic, cruise, air-to-air, and surface-to-air missiles for the PLA and for export has likely been enhanced by upgrades to primary final assembly and rocket motor production facilities over the past few years. China's space launch vehicle industry is expanding to support satellite launch services and the manned space program. The majority of China's missile programs, including its ballistic and cruise missile systems, are comparable to other international top-tier producers, while its surface-to-air missile systems lag behind global leaders. China's missile industry modernization efforts have positioned it well for the foreseeable future.

Naval/Shipbuilding Industry. Shipyard expansion and modernization have increased China's shipbuilding capacity and capability, generating benefits for all types of military projects, including submarines, surface combatants, naval aviation, and sealift assets. China continues to invest in foreign suppliers for some propulsion units, but is becoming increasingly self-reliant. China commissioned its first aircraft carrier, the *Liaoning*, a renovated Russian KUZNETSOV-class hull, in September 2012. China is among the top ship-producing nations in the world and is currently pursuing an indigenous aircraft carrier program. To date, China has not produced a non-carrier surface combatant larger than a destroyer, but is outfitting theses ships with increasingly sophisticated anti-surface, -air and –subsurface defensive and offensive capabilities. China is using more sophisticated ship design and construction program management techniques and software, and it is improving in most areas of the maritime sector.

Armament Industry. There have been production capacity advances in almost every area of PLA ground forces systems, including production of new tanks, armored personnel carriers, air defense artillery systems, and artillery pieces. However, China still relies on foreign acquisition to fill gaps in select critical technical capabilities, such as turbine aircraft engines. China is capable of producing ground weapons systems at or near world standards however, quality concerns persist with some export equipment.

Aviation Industry. China's commercial and military aviation industries have advanced to indigenously produce improved versions of older aircraft and modern fourth-to-fifth generation fighters and attack helicopters. China's commercial aircraft industry has invested in high-precision and technologically advanced machine tools, avionics, and other components that can also be used in the production of military aircraft. However, production in the aircraft industry will be limited by its reliance on foreign sourcing for dependable, proven aircraft engines, as well as a continued lack of skilled personnel and facilities. Infrastructure and experience for the production of large-body commercial and military aircraft are believed to be limited, but growing with new investments. China is developing fourth and fifth generation aircraft that incorporate stealth and low-observable technologies (including carbon fiber and other specialty materials), and it is pursuing an indigenous heavy-lift military transport. Although China is modernizing its aviation industry, it lags behind in the production of reliable high performance aircraft engines.

Foreign Technology Acquisition. Key areas where China continues to supplement indigenous military modernization efforts through targeted foreign technologies include engines for aircraft and tanks, solid state electronics and micro processors, guidance and control systems, and enabling technologies such as cutting-edge precision machine tools, advanced diagnostic and forensic equipment, and computer-assisted design, manufacturing and engineering. China often pursues these foreign technologies for the purpose of reverse engineering or to supplement indigenous military modernization efforts.

Russia has been China's primary weapons and materiel provider, selling China advanced fighter aircraft, helicopters, missile systems, submarines, and destroyers. Relying on Russian components for several of its production programs, China purchased production rights to Russian weapon designs. Though still committed to filling capability gaps with Russian equipment, this trend is changing as China becomes more self-sufficient in research, development, and production.

Science and Technology Development Goals Through 2020. China's *National Medium- and Long-Term Program for Science and Technology Development* (2006-2020), issued by the State Council in February 2006, seeks to transform China into an "innovation-oriented society by 2020." The plan defines China's science and technology focus in terms of "basic research," "leading-edge technologies," "key fields and priority subjects," and "major special items," all of which have military applications.

Basic Research. As part of a broad effort to expand basic research capabilities, China identified five areas that have military applications as major strategic needs or science research plans requiring active government involvement and funding:

> Material design and preparation;

> Manufacturing in extreme environmental conditions;

> Aeronautic and astronautic mechanics;

> Information technology development; and

> Nanotechnology research.

In nanotechnology, China has progressed from virtually no research or funding in 2002 to being a close second to the United States in total government investment.

Leading-edge Technologies. China is focusing on the following technologies for rapid development:

> Information Technology: Priorities include intelligent perception technologies, ad hoc networks, and virtual reality technologies;

> New Materials: Priorities include smart materials and structures, high-temperature superconducting technologies, and highly efficient energy materials technologies;

> Advanced Manufacturing: Priorities include extreme manufacturing technologies and intelligent service advanced machine tools;

> Advanced Energy Technologies: Priorities include hydrogen energy and fuel cell technologies, alternative fuels, and advanced vehicle technologies;

> Marine Technologies: Priorities include three-dimensional maritime environmental monitoring technologies, fast, multi-parameter ocean floor survey technologies, and deep-sea operations technologies; and

> Laser and Aerospace Technologies: Priorities include development of chemical and solid laser state technologies to ultimately field a weapons-grade system from ground-based and airborne platforms.

Key Fields and Priority Subjects. China has identified certain industries and technology groups with potential to provide technological breakthroughs, remove technical obstacles across industries, and improve international competitiveness. Specifically, China's defense industries are pursuing advanced manufacturing, information technology, and defense technologies. Examples include radar, counter-space capabilities, secure C4ISR, smart materials, and low-observable technologies.

Major Special Items. China has also identified 16 "major special items" for which it plans to develop or expand indigenous capabilities. These include core electronic components, high-end universal chips and operating system software, very large-scale integrated circuit manufacturing, next-generation broadband wireless mobile communications, high-grade numerically controlled machine tools, large aircraft, high-resolution satellites, and lunar exploration.

Foreign Arms Acquisition. China seeks some high-tech components and certain major end items that it has difficulty producing domestically, particularly from Russia. China is pursuing advanced Russian defense equipment such as the SA-21 (S-400) surface-to-air missile system and Su-35 fighter aircraft. Between 2011 and 2012, Russia agreed to sell China IL-76 transport aircraft and Mi-171 helicopters. Russia's concerns about intellectual property protections will affect the types and quantities of advanced arms or associated production technologies it is willing to transfer to China. China also has signed significant purchase contracts with Ukraine in recent years, including contracts for assault hovercraft and aircraft engines.

Espionage Supporting Military Modernization. China utilizes a large, well-organized network of enterprises, defense factories, affiliated research institutes, and computer network operations to facilitate the collection of sensitive information and export-controlled technology, as well as basic research and science that supports U.S. defense system modernization. Many of the organizations comprising China's military-industrial complex have both military and civilian research and development functions. This network of government-affiliated companies and research institutes often enables the PLA to access sensitive and dual-use technologies or knowledgeable experts under the guise of civilian research and development. The enterprises and institutes accomplish this through technology conferences and symposia, legitimate contracts and joint commercial ventures, partnerships with foreign firms, and joint development of specific technologies.

As in previous years, China utilized its intelligence services and employed other illicit approaches that involve violations of U.S. laws and export controls to obtain key national security technologies, controlled equipment, and other materials not readily obtainable through commercial means or academia. Based on investigations conducted by the law enforcement agencies of the Department of Defense, Department of Justice, Department of Homeland Security, and Department of Commerce, China continues to engage in activities designed to support military procurement and modernization. These include economic espionage, theft of trade secrets, export control violations, and technology transfer.

> In August 2010, Noshir Gowadia was convicted of providing China with classified U.S. defense technology. This assisted China in developing a low-signature cruise missile exhaust system capable of rendering a cruise missile resistant to detection by infrared missiles.

> In September 2010, Chi Tong Kuok was convicted for conspiracy to illegally export U.S. military encryption technology and smuggle it to Macau and Hong Kong. The relevant technology included encryption, communications equipment, and Global Positioning System (GPS)

equipment used by U.S. and NATO forces.

> In September 2010, Xian Hongwei and Li Li were arrested in Hungary and later extradited to the United States for conspiring to procure thousands of radiation-hardened Programmable Read-Only Microchips, classified as defense items and used in satellite systems, for the China Aerospace and Technology Corporation. Both defendants pleaded guilty and were sentenced in September 2011 to two years in prison.

> In January 2012, Yang Bin was arrested in Bulgaria and later extradited to the United States based on a December 2011 criminal indictment related to the attempted export of military-grade accelerometers used in "smart" munitions, aircraft, and missiles.

> In July 2012, Zhang Zhaowei, a naturalized Canadian citizen, was arrested while entering the United States, based on a sealed January 2011 indictment alleging Zhang attempted to illegally acquire and export military gyroscopes used in unmanned aerial systems and for tactical missile guidance.

> In September 2012, Zhang Mingsuan was arrested in the United States and indicted after attempting to acquire up to two tons of aerospace-grade carbon fiber. In a recorded conversation, Zhang claimed he urgently needed the fiber in connection with a scheduled Chinese fighter plane test flight.

In addition, multiple cases identified since 2009 involved individuals procuring and exporting export controlled items to China. These efforts included attempts to procure and export radiation-hardened programmable semiconductors and computer circuits used in satellites, restricted microwave amplifiers used in communications and radar equipment, export-restricted technical data, and thermal imaging cameras. There were also at least two cases in 2011 in which U.S. companies working on Department of Defense contracts subcontracted manufacturing work on small arms and replacement parts to Chinese companies in violation of the Arms Export Control Act.

China's Arms Exports

From 2007 to 2011, China signed approximately $11 billion in agreements for conventional weapons systems worldwide, ranging from general purpose materiel to major weapons systems. In 2012 and the coming years, China's arms exports will likely increase modestly as China's domestic defense industry improves. Chinese defense firms are marketing and selling arms throughout the world with the bulk of their sales to Asia and the Middle East/North Africa. In 2012, China unveiled the Yi Long tactical unmanned aerial vehicle, which will probably be marketed to developing countries.

> Pakistan remains China's primary customer for conventional weapons. China engages in both arms sales and defense industrial cooperation with Islamabad, including co-production of the JF-17 fighter aircraft, F-22P frigates with helicopters, K-8 jet trainers, F-7 fighter aircraft, early warning and control aircraft, tanks, air-to-air missiles, anti-ship cruise missiles, and cooperation on main battle tank production.

> Sub-Saharan African countries view China as a provider of low-cost weapons with fewer political strings attached compared to other international arms suppliers. China uses arms sales as part of a multifaceted approach to promote trade, secure access to natural resources, and extend its influence in the region.

5

FORCE MODERNIZATION FOR A TAIWAN CONTINGENCY

OVERVIEW

Security in the Taiwan Strait is largely a function of dynamic interactions between and among mainland China, Taiwan, and the United States. China's strategy toward Taiwan continues to be influenced by what it sees as positive developments in Taiwan's political situation and approach to engagement with Beijing. However, China's overall strategy continues to incorporate elements of persuasion and coercion to deter or repress the development of political attitudes in Taiwan favoring independence. The two sides made progress in expanding cross-Strait trade/economic links and people-to-people contacts; China addressed in limited terms Taiwan's expressed desire for greater international space through its decision not to oppose Taiwan's meaningful participation in the World Health Assembly.

Alongside positive public statements about the Taiwan Strait situation from top leaders in China following the re-election of Taiwan President Ma Ying-jeou in 2012, however, there have been no signs that China's military disposition opposite Taiwan has changed significantly. The PLA has developed and deployed military capabilities to coerce Taiwan or to attempt an invasion, if necessary. These improvements pose major challenges to Taiwan's security, which has been based historically upon the PLA's inability to project power across the 100 nm Taiwan Strait, natural geographic advantages of island defense, Taiwan's armed forces' technological superiority, and the possibility of U.S. intervention.

CHINA'S STRATEGY IN THE TAIWAN STRAIT

China appears prepared to defer the use of force, as long as it believes that unification over the long-term remains possible and the costs of conflict outweigh the benefits. China argues that the credible threat to use force is essential to maintain the conditions for political progress, and to prevent Taiwan from making moves toward *de jure* independence. China has refused for decades to renounce the use of force to resolve the Taiwan issue, despite simultaneously professing its desire for peaceful unification under the principle of "one country, two systems."

The circumstances under which the mainland has historically warned it would use force have evolved over time in response to the island's declarations of political status, changes in PLA capabilities, and China's view of Taiwan's relations with other countries. These circumstances, or "red lines," have included:

> Formal declaration of Taiwan independence;

> Undefined moves toward Taiwan independence;

> Internal unrest on Taiwan;

> Taiwan's acquisition of nuclear weapons;

> Indefinite delays in the resumption of cross-Strait dialogue on unification;

> Foreign intervention in Taiwan's internal affairs; and

> Foreign troops stationed on Taiwan.

Article 8 of the March 2005 "Anti-Secession Law" states that China may use "non-peaceful means" if "secessionist forces ... cause the fact of Taiwan's secession from China;" if "major incidents entailing Taiwan's secession" occur; or, if "possibilities for peaceful reunification" are exhausted. The ambiguity of these "redlines" preserves China's flexibility.

CHINA'S COURSES OF ACTION AGAINST TAIWAN

The PLA is capable of increasingly sophisticated military action against Taiwan. It is possible China would first pursue a measured approach characterized by signaling its readiness to use force, followed by a deliberate buildup of force to optimize the speed of engagement over strategic deception. Another option is that China would sacrifice overt, large-scale preparations in favor of surprise to force rapid military and/or political resolution before other countries could respond. If a quick resolution is not possible, China would seek to:

> Deter potential U.S. intervention;

> Failing that, delay intervention and seek victory in an asymmetric, limited, quick war; and,

> Fight to a standstill and pursue a political settlement after a protracted conflict.

Maritime Quarantine or Blockade. In addition to direct military engagement, PLA writings describe potential alternative solutions—air blockades, missile attacks, and mining to force capitulation. China could declare that ships en route to Taiwan must stop in mainland ports for inspection and/or transshipment prior to transiting to Taiwan ports. China could also attempt the equivalent of a blockade by declaring exercise or missile closure areas in approaches to ports, in effect closing port access and diverting merchant traffic. The PLA employed this method during the 1995-96 missile firings and live-fire exercises. There is a risk, however, that China would underestimate the degree to which any attempt to limit maritime traffic to and from Taiwan would trigger countervailing international pressure and military escalation. China today probably could not enforce a full military blockade, particularly if a major naval power intervened. However, its ability to do so will improve significantly over the next five to ten years.

Limited Force or Coercive Options. China might use a variety of disruptive, punitive, or lethal military actions in a limited campaign against Taiwan, likely in conjunction with overt and clandestine economic and political activities. Such a campaign could include computer network or limited kinetic attacks against Taiwan's political, military, and economic infrastructure to induce fear in Taiwan and degrade the populace's confidence in the Taiwan leadership. Similarly, PLA special operations forces could infiltrate Taiwan and conduct attacks against infrastructure or leadership targets.

Air and Missile Campaign. Limited SRBM attacks and precision strikes against air defense systems, including air bases, radar sites, missiles, space assets, and communications facilities, could be conducted in an attempt to degrade Taiwan's defenses, neutralize Taiwan's leadership, or break the Taiwan people's will to fight.

Amphibious Invasion. Publicly available Chinese writings describe different operational concepts for amphibious invasion. The most prominent of these, the Joint Island Landing Campaign, envisions a complex operation relying on coordinated, interlocking campaigns for logistics, air and naval support, and EW. The objective would be to break through or circumvent shore defenses, establish and build a beachhead, transport personnel and materiel to designated landing sites in the north or south of Taiwan's western coastline, and launch attacks to seize and occupy key targets and/or the entire island.

The PLA is capable of accomplishing various amphibious operations short of a full-scale invasion of Taiwan. With few overt military preparations beyond routine training, China could launch an invasion of small Taiwan-held islands in the South China Sea such as Pratas or Itu Aba. A PLA invasion of a medium-sized, better defended offshore island such as Matsu or Jinmen is within China's capabilities. Such an invasion would demonstrate military capability and political resolve while achieving tangible territorial gain and simultaneously showing some measure of restraint. However, this kind of operation includes significant, if not prohibitive, political risk because it could galvanize pro-independence sentiment on Taiwan and generate international opposition.

Large-scale amphibious invasion is one of the most complicated and difficult military operations. Success depends upon air and sea superiority, rapid buildup and sustainment of supplies on shore, and uninterrupted support. An attempt to invade Taiwan would strain China's armed forces and invite international intervention. These stresses, combined with China's combat force attrition and the complexity of urban warfare and counterinsurgency (assuming a successful landing and breakout), make amphibious invasion of Taiwan a significant political and military risk. Taiwan's investments to harden infrastructure and strengthen defensive capabilities could also decrease China's ability to achieve its objectives. Moreover, China does not appear to be building the conventional amphibious lift required to support such a campaign.

THE PLA'S CURRENT POSTURE FOR A TAIWAN CONFLICT

Preparation for a Taiwan conflict with the possibility of U.S. intervention has largely dominated China's military modernization program. Despite decreased cross-strait tensions since 2008, Taiwan remains a primary military focus.

Missile Forces. The Second Artillery is prepared to conduct SRBM attacks and precision strikes against Taiwan's air defense systems, air bases, radar sites, missiles, space assets, C2 and communications facilities, in an attempt to degrade Taiwan's defenses, neutralize Taiwan's leadership, or break the public's will to fight.

Air Forces. The PLA Air Force has maintained a force posture that provides it with a variety of capabilities to leverage against Taiwan in a contingency. First, it has stationed a large number of advanced aircraft within an unrefueled range of Taiwan, providing them with a significant capability to conduct air superiority and ground attack operations against Taiwan. Second, a number of long-range air defense systems provide a strong layer of defense of China's mainland against a counterattack. Third, China's development of support aircraft provide it improved ISR to support PLA Air Force operations in a contingency.

Navy Forces. The PLA Navy is improving anti-air and anti-surface warfare capabilities, developing a credible at-sea nuclear deterrent, and introducing new platforms that are positioned to strike Taiwan in a cross-Strait conflict. The additional attack submarines, multi-mission surface combatants, and fourth-generation naval aircraft entering the force are designed to achieve sea superiority within the first island chain and counter any potential third party intervention in a Taiwan conflict. The PLA Navy currently lacks the massive amphibious lift capacity that a large-scale invasion of Taiwan would require.

Ground Forces. Increasingly armed with more modern systems such as armed attack helicopters, the PLA ground forces are conducting joint training exercises that will prepare them for a Taiwan invasion scenario. Training, including amphibious landing training, is often conducted under realistic conditions, including all-weather and at night. Improved networks provide real-time data transmissions within and between units, enabling better command and control during operations. Additionally, the PLA Army's ongoing fielding of advanced air defense equipment is significantly enhancing the self defense of key command and control elements and other critical assets assessed as likely tasked for potential use against Taiwan. As the number of these new systems grows in the PLA ground forces, the ability of an amphibious invasion force to successfully defend cross-Strait amphibious lodgments against counterattacks by both legacy and advanced weaponry will inevitably increase.

TAIWAN'S DEFENSIVE CAPABILITIES

Taiwan has historically relied upon multiple military variables to deter PLA aggression: the PLA's inability to project sufficient power across the 100 mile Taiwan Strait, the Taiwan military's technological superiority, and the inherent geographic advantages of island defense. China's increasingly modern weapons and platforms (more than 1,100 ballistic missiles, an anti-ship ballistic missile program, ships and submarines, combat aircraft, and improved C4ISR capabilities) have largely negated many of these factors.

Taiwan has taken important steps to build its war reserve stocks, grow its defense industrial base, improve joint operations and crisis response capabilities, and increase its officer and noncommissioned officer (NCO) corps. These improvements partially address Taiwan's eroding defensive advantages. Taiwan is following through with its transition to a volunteer military and reducing its active military end-strength from 275,000 to 215,000 personnel to create a "small but smart and strong force." Under this plan, which is slated for completion by December 2014, the cost savings from a smaller force will free up resources to increase volunteer salaries and benefits, although these savings are not sufficient to cover the costs of volunteers. However, the transition has led to additional personnel costs needed to attract and retain personnel under the volunteer system, diverting funds from foreign and indigenous acquisition programs, as well as near-term training and readiness. The actual number of active-duty service members is approximately 235,000 – well below the 275,000 currently

authorized. In addition, Taiwan military spending has dropped to approximately 2 percent of GDP – well below President Ma's pledge of 3 percent. China's official defense budget is about 10 times that of Taiwan. Realizing that Taiwan cannot match China's military spending, Taiwan is working to integrate innovative and asymmetric measures into its defense planning in order to counter-balance China's growing capabilities.

U.S. policy toward Taiwan derives from its One-China Policy, based on the three Joint Communiqués and the Taiwan Relations Act (TRA). U.S. policy opposes any unilateral changes to the status quo in the Taiwan Strait by either side. The United States continues to support peaceful resolution of cross-Strait differences in a manner acceptable to the people on both sides.

Consistent with the TRA, the United States has helped to maintain peace, security, and stability in the Taiwan Strait by providing defense articles and services to enable Taiwan to maintain a sufficient self defense capability. To this end, the United States has announced more than $12 billion in arms sales to Taiwan since 2010. This includes, most recently, in September 2011, the U.S. announcement of its intent to sell to Taiwan $5.85 billion worth of defensive arms and equipment, including an advanced retrofit program for Taiwan's F-16 A/B fighter jets, training, and spare parts for Taiwan's air force.

6

U.S.-CHINA
MILITARY-TO-MILITARY CONTACTS

STRATEGY FOR ENGAGEMENT

Over the past two decades, the PRC has steadily transformed a poorly equipped, ground forces-centric military into a more capable force that is assuming diverse missions well beyond China's shores. Given this trajectory, the need for a robust U.S.-China military-to-military relationship that builds trust and helps manage friction continues to grow. During their January 2011 summit, U.S. President Barack Obama and PRC President Hu Jintao jointly affirmed that a "healthy, stable, and reliable military-to-military relationship is an essential part of [their] shared vision for a positive, cooperative, and comprehensive U.S. China relationship." Both sides have repeatedly endorsed this objective.

The fundamental purpose for two countries to conduct military-to-military relations is to gain a better understanding of how each side thinks about the role and use of military power in achieving political and strategic objectives. It is precisely during periods of tension when a working relationship is most important. Over the long term, a fully functioning relationship should help both parties develop a more acute awareness of the potential for cooperation and competition. Sustained and substantive military-to-military contacts at all levels can help reduce miscommunication, misunderstanding, and the risks of miscalculation.

The United States bases its contacts and exchanges with China's military on the principles of mutual respect, mutual trust, reciprocity, mutual interest, continuous dialogue, and mutual risk reduction. The Department of Defense conducts them in a manner consistent with the provisions of Section 1201 of the National Defense Authorization Act (NDAA) for Fiscal Year 2000, which provide the Secretary of Defense sufficient latitude to develop a program of exchanges with China that supports U.S. national interests.

The complexity of the security environment both in the Asia-Pacific region and globally, calls for a continuous dialogue between the armed forces of the United States and China. The U.S. position is that our engagement with China should expand cooperation in areas of mutual interest, provide a forum to candidly address areas of disagreement and improve mutual understanding. The United States sees value in sustained and reliable military ties and regards the military relationship as an integral component of a comprehensive U.S.-China relationship.

Sustained military engagement underpins U.S. policy objectives of promoting China's development in a manner consistent with international rules and norms and that contributes to regional and global problem-solving. The U.S. National Defense Strategy emphasizes that U.S. defense interaction with China will be long-term and multi-dimensional.

U.S. military-to-military engagement with China serves three general purposes in support of the broader relationship. First, it allows the U.S. and PRC militaries to build cooperative capacity. This is achieved through activities that enhance or facilitate our ability to interact at a tactical or operational level. Second, engagement fosters understanding of each others' military institutions in ways that dispel misconceptions and encourage common ground for dialogue. Third, military engagement allows senior leaders to address the global security environment and relevant challenges. These interactions can facilitate common approaches to challenges and serves as a bridge to build more productive working relationships.

MILITARY-TO-MILITARY ENGAGEMENT IN 2012 - HIGHLIGHTS

2012 was a year of positive momentum in the military relationship between the United States and China. Although the 2012 military-to-military engagement plan was not finalized until April 2012, PRC Vice President Xi Jinping's successful visit to the Pentagon and meeting with U.S. Secretary of Defense Panetta in February set the tone for a positive atmosphere that continued through the year. Although both nations underwent political transitions in November, the robust schedule of engagements proceeded without interruption – selected visits are highlighted

below (see complete list of 2012 engagements at Appendix II).

High Level Visits. Along with PRC Vice President Xi Jinping's February visit to the United States, PRC Minister of National Defense General Liang Guanglie traveled to the United States in May, visiting San Francisco; Naval Air Station, San Diego; Washington, DC; SOUTHCOM Headquarters in Miami; Camp Lejeune, North Carolina; Ft. Benning, Georgia; and the U.S. Military Academy at West Point.

PACOM Commander Admiral Samuel Locklear visited China in June, where he had meetings in Beijing and visited the Guangzhou Military Region Headquarters, observed tank live fire demonstrations in Guilin, and received briefings at the South Sea Fleet Command Headquarters in Zhanjiang and toured a PLA Navy destroyer.

In August, PRC Deputy Chief of the General Staff, General Cai Yingting, visited the United States, making stops in New York; Washington, DC; Fort Hood, TX; and PACOM Headquarters in Honolulu.

Secretary Panetta visited China in September, where he met with senior military and civilian leaders in Beijing and gave an address to cadets at the PLA's Armed Forces Engineering Academy (several of whom he shared lunch with afterward). Secretary of Defense Panetta then traveled south to Qingdao, where he visited China's North Sea Fleet headquarters and toured a SONG-class diesel electric submarine and a JIANGKAI II-class guided missile frigate. Secretary of Defense Panetta invited China to participate in RIM OF THE PACIFIC (RIMPAC), PACIFIC PARTNERSHIP, and PACIFIC ANGEL exercises.

Finally, at the end of November 2012, Secretary of the Navy Ray Mabus conducted a visit to China that included meetings in Beijing and visits to the PLA Navy's bases in Zhoushan and Daxie Dao, where he toured the *Peace Ark* hospital ship, a JIANGKAI II-class guided missile frigate, and a YUAN-class SSP submarine.

Recurrent Exchanges. A full slate of recurrent exchanges was also conducted in 2012. These events form the backbone of defense policy-level discussions for the two nations and serve as a more regularized, routine mechanism for dialogue than high-level visits, with their less-predictable schedules.

In May, on the margins of the Strategic and Economic Dialogue (S&ED) in Beijing, Under Secretary of Defense for Policy Dr. James Miller participated in the Department of State-led second annual Strategic Security Dialogue (SSD). Under Secretary Miller also led the Department of Defense delegation to the S&ED, where he spoke at the final security track plenary session (hosted by U.S. Secretary of State Hillary Clinton and PRC State Councilor Dai Bingguo) on the state of U.S.-China military-to-military relations.

Under Secretary Miller's PRC counterpart, then-Deputy Chief of the General Staff General Ma Xiaotian, also participated in both the SSD and the S&ED.

The PACOM-led Military Maritime Consultative Agreement (MMCA) plenary session (focused on maritime safety) took place in Qingdao in September, with preparatory working group meeting in June (future meetings may also focus on safe air intercept practices).

In October 2012, the two sides conducted the annual Defensive Policy Coordination Talks (DPCTs) at the Pentagon, with maritime safety/security and regional/global security issues the focus of the agenda. In addition to beginning negotiations for the 2013 military-to-military engagement plant, the DPCTs set the stage for Under Secretary Miller to conduct the annual Defense Consultative Talks (DCTs) in December at the Pentagon. The DCTs are the highest-level annual defense dialogue between the United States and China.

Academic, Functional Exchanges. In June 2012, 29 PLA generals, primarily from the ground forces, visited the United States as part of a delegation of students in the strategic "Dragons" course at the PLA National Defense University (NDU). The U.S. NDU "Capstone" course conducted a reciprocal visit to China the following month.

In August, a PLA Civilian Personnel System delegation visited the United States (and Canada) to learn more about integration of civilian and military personnel in the Department of Defense. The visit increased mutual institutional understanding and covered issues including promotion systems, ranking equivalency, casualty compensation, and incorporating retired military personnel into civilian roles.

In September, just days before Secretary of Defense Panetta's visit to China, the United States and China conducted their first bilateral counter-piracy exercise in the Gulf of Aden.

In November 2012, the PRC hosted experts from the U.S. Army Pacific for an annual Disaster Management Exchange (DME), which included a table-top exercise where both sides discussed possible responses to an earthquake in a third country.

In December 2012, the PACOM Command Surgeon led a military medical delegation to China, the first delegation of its kind, in an effort to chart out more robust cooperation.

PLANNING FOR MILITARY-TO-MILITARY ENGAGEMENTS IN 2013

Planning for 2013 military-to-military engagements began mid-year 2012 and continued during the DPCTs in October. As this report went to print, the 2013 plan had been agreed to in principle.

SPECIAL TOPIC: SPACE-BASED IMAGING AND REMOTE SENSING

China has developed a large constellation of imaging and remote sensing satellites under a variety of mission families. These satellites can support military objectives by providing situational awareness of foreign military force deployments, critical infrastructure, and targets of political significance. Since 2006, China has conducted 16 Yaogan remote sensing satellite launches. The Yaogan satellites conduct scientific experiments, carry out surveys on land resources, estimate crop yield, and support natural disaster reduction and prevention. Additionally, China has launched two Tianhui satellites designed to conduct scientific experiments and support land resource surveys and territory mapping with a stereoscopic imaging payload. China has three Huanjing disaster monitoring satellites currently on orbit (the third of which was launched in November 2012). The Ziyuan series of satellites are used for earth resources, cartography, surveying, and monitoring. China also operates the Haiyang ocean monitoring constellation and Fengyun weather satellites in low Earth and geosynchronous orbits. China will continue to increase its on-orbit constellation with the planned launch of 100 satellites through 2015. These launches include imaging, remote sensing, navigation, communication, and scientific satellites, as well as manned spacecraft.

SPECIAL TOPIC: CHINA'S FIRST AIRCRAFT CARRIER

The most significant development in the PLA Navy over the past year has been the sea trials and commissioning of China's first aircraft carrier, the *Liaoning*. The *Liaoning* was commissioned and entered service with the PLA Navy on September 25, 2012. The carrier most likely will conduct extensive local operations focusing on shipboard training, carrier aircraft integration, and carrier formation training before reaching an operational effectiveness in three to four years. The carrier could operate in the East and South China Seas in the nearer term and may be used for other mission sets as needed.

The carrier will most likely be based at Yuchi in the Qingdao area in the near term, although Sanya Naval Base on Hainan Island is also a possibility, particularly after an operational air wing is formed. The base under construction at Yuchi features a deep draft harbor with replenishment, repair, and maintenance facilities. The Qingdao area also supports nearby airfields for aircraft maintenance and repair.

The J-15 aircraft conducted its first takeoffs and landings from the *Liaoning* on November 26, 2012. Subsequently, at least two aircraft conducted multiple landings and takeoffs from the ship. The J-15 carrier-based fighter is the Chinese version of the Russian Su-33. The J-15 is designed for ski-jump takeoffs and arrested landings, as required by the configuration of the *Liaoning*. Although the J-15 has a land-based combat radius of 1200 km, the aircraft will be limited in range and armament when operating from the carrier, due to limits imposed by the ski-jump takeoff and arrested carrier landings.

The formation of carrier battle groups will enable the PLA Navy to conduct comprehensive operations and enhance its long-range operational capabilities. Although reports have surfaced regarding the construction of a second Chinese aircraft carrier in Shanghai, the Chinese Ministry of National Defense has dismissed these claims.

SPECIAL TOPIC: PLA AIR FORCE STEALTH AIRCRAFT

The PLA seeks to develop aircraft with low observable features, advanced avionics, super-cruise engines, and stealth applications, as demonstrated by the January 2011 flight test of the J-20 prototype and recent observations of a second indigenously-produced aircraft with stealth features. China seeks to develop these advanced aircraft to improve its regional airpower projection capabilities and strengthen its ability to strike regional airbases and facilities. China's first fifth generation fighter is not expected to enter service prior to 2018, and China faces numerous challenges to achieving full operational capability, including developing high-performance jet engines.

The PLA Air Force has observed foreign military employment of stealth aircraft and views this technology as a core capability in its transformation from a predominantly territorial air force to one capable of conducting offensive and defensive operations. The PLA Air Force also perceives there is an imbalance between offensive and defensive operations due to advances in stealth aircraft and related technologies with stealth aircraft providing an offensive operational advantage that denies an adversary the time to mobilize and conduct defensive operations. The PLA Air Force also sees the offensive advantage to combining an aircraft's stealthy features with information systems that enhance situational awareness and improve coordination of forces during combat.

The development of stealth aircraft incorporated with advanced fifth generation capabilities, including super-cruise engines and advanced avionics, would make the aircraft capable of supporting a variety of tactical and regional missions. Furthermore, stealth aircraft the size of China's J-20 could be used as a multi-role fighter to strike ground targets within the region in addition to supporting air superiority missions beyond China's borders. Although China's second developmental fifth generation fighter is smaller in size than the J-20, this aircraft (tentatively identified as the J-31) may be designed for multi-role missions, providing China with a second stealth platform for regional operations. In addition to manned fighter aircraft, the PLA Air Force also views stealth technology as integral to unmanned aircraft, specifically those with an air-to-ground role, as this technology will improve the system's ability to penetrate heavily protected targets.

The PLA recognizes the technological challenges posed by the next generation of advanced fighters, and has concerns about its ability to counter U.S. 5th generation aircraft, such as the F-22 and F-35. In response, the PLA Air Force has emphasized the need to develop systems and training to defend against the employment of foreign stealth technology in combat. In addition, the PLA Air Force believes that it should not focus solely on defense against stealth technology, but must also emphasize offensive capabilities to counter an adversary's use of stealth technology, to include the use of long-range attack capabilities to destroy enemy aircraft on the ground.

SPECIAL TOPIC: PLA INTEGRATED AIR DEFENSES

China has developed a national integrated air defense system (IADS) to defend key strategic cities and borders, territorial claims, and forces against threats from the air. Overall, China's IADS represents a multilayered defense consisting of weapons systems, radars and C4ISR platforms working together to counter multiple types of air threats at various ranges and altitudes. One of China's primary goals is to defend against precision strike munitions such as cruise and ballistic missiles, especially those launched from long distances. In order to counter precision strike munitions, China has developed advanced long-range SAM systems, airborne early warning platforms, and C2 networks. Defense against stealth aircraft and unmanned aerial vehicles is also a growing priority. Another aspect of China's IADS development is the deployment of land-based air defense brigades beyond the eastern coast of China and improving the air defense of China's naval fleets in the ECS and SCS. This is part of China's longstanding effort to expand its capabilities from focusing on territorial defense to supporting both defensive and offensive operations.

Air Defense Weapons. China's air force and navy employ land- and sea-based SAMs and antiaircraft artillery (AAA) and its ground forces employ short- and medium-range SAMs and AAA in extensive numbers. The PLA Air Force employs one of the largest forces of advanced long-range SAM systems in the world, including SA-20 battalions acquired from Russia and domestically-produced HQ-9 battalions. China has shown interest in acquiring Russia's newest long-range SAM, the S-400 TRIUMF, but a contract has not been signed yet and Russian officials have stated China would not receive the S-400 until at least 2017. This SAM can target aircraft, cruise missiles, and tactical and medium-range ballistic missiles.

Early Warning Network. Another element of China's multilayered IADS is its extensive ground-based radar network. In the past, this ground-based early warning network and China's Russian-acquired SAMs primarily protected Beijing and other key strategic locations in the eastern part of the country. China has since developed the KONGJING-2000 (KJ-2000) airborne early warning aircraft to provide coverage at long ranges and low altitudes for faster response and command targeting to weapons systems. In the future China may expand its national early warning network to protect China's territorial air space and waters farther from the mainland, as well as to provide space defense. This effort would include China's growing constellations of reconnaissance, data relay, navigation, and communications satellites. China is also improving reconnaissance technologies to include infrared, multiple-spectrum, pulsed doppler, phased array, and passive detection. Over-the-horizon skywave radar is also an important component of China's improvement in its strategic early warning capabilities.

C4ISR Network. China's IADS also includes a C4ISR network to connect early warning platforms, SAM and AAA, and command posts in order to improve communication and response time during operations. The network is intended to include battle damage assessment capability. China continues to make progress on command, communication, and control systems. China's air defense brigades are training to use this information network and mobile C2 platforms to connect different types of weapons systems' operations together by sending automated targeting information to them simultaneously. Weapon systems that are geographically separate, in different units, and a mix of older and newer battalions could achieve compatibility through the use of networked C2. China is also using simulation systems to attempt to train for command of air defense operations in realistic operational conditions, including network warfare. China has deployed air defense brigades employing its newest SAM system to the western part of China to train for long-distance mobility and operations in high-altitude conditions, including operations in the conditions of network warfare.

APPENDIX I: MILITARY-TO-MILITARY EXCHANGES

U.S.-CHINA MILITARY-TO-MILITARY CONTACTS FOR 2012	
HIGH-LEVEL VISITS TO CHINA	*Month (2012)*
USPACOM Commander to China	June
Secretary of Defense to China	September
Secretary of the Navy to China	November
HIGH-LEVEL VISITS TO UNITED STATES	
PRC Minister of Defense to United States	May
PRC Deputy Chief of the General Staff for Strategic Planning to United States	July
RECURRENT EXCHANGES	
Defense POW/Missing Personnel Office meeting with PLA Archivists	May
Military Maritime Consultative Agreement (MMCA) Working Group in United States	June
MMCA Plenary Session in China	September
Defense Policy Coordination Talks in United States	October
Defense Consultative Talks in United States	December
ACADEMIC EXCHANGES TO UNITED STATES	
PLA University of Science and Technology delegation to United States	April
PRC National Defense University student delegation to United States	June
ACADEMIC EXCHANGES TO CHINA	
National War College student delegation to China	May
National Defense University CAPSTONE Course to China	July
FUNCTIONAL EXCHANGES TO UNITED STATES	
PLA Civilian System Delegation to United States	August
PRC Deputy Chief of Naval Operations Visit to United States	December
FUNCTIONAL EXCHANGES TO CHINA	
U.S. Army Band to China	November
Disaster Management Exchange and Tabletop Exercise in China	November
USPACOM Command Surgeon General Visit to China	December
JOINT EXERCISES	
Gulf of Aden (GOA) Counter-piracy Exercise	September

U.S.-CHINA MILITARY-TO-MILITARY EXCHANGES PLANNED FOR 2013

HIGH-LEVEL VISITS TO CHINA

Chairman of the Joint Chiefs of Staff to China

Chief of Staff of the Air Force to China

Chief of Staff of the Army to China

HIGH-LEVEL VISITS TO UNITED STATES

PRC Vice Chairman of the Central Military Commission or Minister of Defense visit to United States

PRC Chief of Naval Operations to United States

PRC Senior Military Delegation (TBD)

Military Delegation (TBD)

RECURRENT EXCHANGES

MMCA Working Group in China (2x)

MMCA Special Session

MMCA Plenary Session

Disaster Management Exchange

Defense POW/Missing Personnel Office meeting with PLA Archivists

Defense Policy Coordination Talks

Defense Consultative Talks

ACADEMIC EXCHANGES TO UNITED STATES

U.S. National Defense University- PRC National Defense University Strategic Dialogue

PRC National Defense University student delegation to United States (2x)

Academy of Military Science / Army War College Exchange

PLA Navy Command College Student Delegation to United States

PRC Army cadet participation in West Point's International Week/Sandhurst competition

ACADEMIC EXCHANGES TO CHINA

National Defense University President

National Defense University student delegation

National War College Student delegation

U.S. Air War College

U.S. Naval War College student delegation

West Point cadet visit to PLA University of Science and Technology

FUNCTIONAL EXCHANGES TO UNITED STATES

PLA Senior Leader Familiarization Course

Non-Traditional Security Missions Logistics Working Group

Military Lawyer Study Group

PLA Daily Media Delegation

Human Resources Management Study Group

PLA Navy Ship Visit

PLA Medical Department Chief Visit to USPACOM

PLA Observers to LIGHTNING RESCUE 13

PRC Peacekeeping Delegation to Carlisle Barracks, PS

FUNCTIONAL EXCHANGES TO CHINA

USPACOM Mid-level Officer Delegation

U.S. Army Corps of Engineers Delegation

OSD Media and Public Affairs Delegation

U.S. Navy Ship Visit

U.S. Navy Senior Leader Familiarization Course

JOINT EXERCISES

Gulf of Aden Counter-piracy Exercise

Disaster Management Exchange and Humanitarian Assistance/Disaster Relief Exercise

Search and Rescue Exercise in conjunction with ship visit

CHINA'S FOREIGN MILITARY EXCHANGES

Countries Visited by Senior Chinese Military Leaders in 2012

Argentina	India	Poland	Tanzania
Belarus	Latvia	Senegal	Thailand
Bosnia and Herzogovina	Laos	Seychelles	Turkey
	Lithuania	Singapore	Turkmenistan
Burma	Malaysia	Sri Lanka	United States
Cambodia	Mongolia	South Africa	Uzbekistan
Gabon	Pakistan	Tajikistan	

Senior Foreign Military Officials Visiting China in 2012

Australia	Israel	Pakistan	Thailand
Brunei	Kazakhstan	Poland	Togo
Burma	Kyrgyzstan	Russia	Trinidad and Tobago
Central African Republic	Latvia	Singapore	Ukraine
	Lithuania	Slovakia	
Chile	Maldives	South Africa	United States
Croatia	Moldova	Sri Lanka	Uzbekistan
Cuba	New Zealand	Sweden	Vietnam
Germany			Zambia

BILATERAL OR MULTILATERAL MILITARY EXERCISES INVOLVING THE PLA 2007-2012

Year	Exercise Name	Type of Exercise	Participants
	Bilateral and Multilateral Exercises Since 2007		
2007	Aman (Peace) 2007	Search and Rescue	Pakistan
	China-France Friendship 2007	Maritime	France
	China-Spain Friendship 2007	Maritime	Spain
	Cooperation 2007	Counterterrorism	Russia
	Hand-in-Hand 2007	Counterterrorism	India
	Peace Mission 2007	Counterterrorism	Russia, Kazakhstan, Kyrgyzstan, Tajikistan, Uzbekistan
	Strike 2007	Counterterrorism	Thailand
	Western Pacific Naval Symposium	Search and Rescue	United States, France, Japan, Australia, New Zealand, India, Pakistan, ROK, Singapore
	Unnamed	Maritime	India
	Unnamed	Search and Rescue	Australia, New Zealand
2008	Hand-in-Hand 2008	Counterterrorism	India
	Strike 2008	Counterterrorism	Thailand
2009	Aman (Peace) 2009	Maritime	Hosted by Pakistan (38 countries participated)
	Cooperation 2009	Counterterrorism	Singapore
	Country-Gate Sharp Sword 2009	Counterterrorism	Russia
	Peace Angel 2009	Medical	Gabon
	Peace Keeping Mission 2009	Peacekeeping Operations	Mongolia
	Peace Mission 2009	Counterterrorism	Russia
	Peace Shield 2009	Counter-piracy	Russia
	Unnamed	Maritime	Singapore
2010	Blue Strike/Blue Assault 2010	Counterterrorism	Thailand
	Cooperation 2010	Counterterrorism	Singapore
	Friendship 2010	Counterterrorism	Pakistan
	Friendship Action 2010	Ground (Mountain Warfare)	Romania
	Peace Angel 2010	Medical	Peru
	Peace Mission 2010	Counterterrorism	Russia, Kazakhstan, Kyrgyzstan, Tajikistan
	Strike 2010	Counterterrorism	Thailand
	Unnamed	Search and Rescue	Australia
	Unnamed	Maritime	New Zealand
	Unnamed	Counter-piracy	South Korea
	Unnamed	Search and Rescue	Taiwan
	Unnamed	Air	Turkey
	Unnamed	Ground	Turkey
	Unnamed	Search and Rescue	Vietnam

	Unnamed	Joint Border Patrol	Kazakhstan
	Shaheen 1	Air Exercise	Pakistan
2011	Tian Shan-2 2011	Counterterrorism	Kazakhstan, Kyrgyzstan, Russia, Tajikistan, Uzbekistan
	Aman (Peace) 2011	Maritime	Hosted by Pakistan (39 countries participated)
	Unnamed	Maritime (Counter-piracy)	Tanzania
	Unnamed	Maritime (Counter-piracy)	Pakistan
	Sharp Blade-2011	Special Operations/Counterterrorism	Indonesia
	Unnamed	Maritime	Vietnam
	Unnamed	Airborne	Belarus
	Khan Quest-11	Peacekeeping Operations (observer status)	Mongolia
	Cooperation-2011	Special Operations (Urban Warfare)	Venezuela
	Friendship-IV	Ground (Low Intensity Conflict)	Pakistan
	Cooperation Spirit 2011	Humanitarian Aid/Disaster Relief	Australia
2012	Naval Cooperation 2012	Maritime	Russia
	Unnamed	Counter-piracy	France
	Blue Assault 2012	Maritime (Amphibious Assault)	Thailand
	Peace Mission 2012	Counterterrorism	Kazakhstan, Kyrgyzstan, Russia, Tajikistan, Uzbekistan
	Sharp Knife 2012	Counterterrorism	Indonesia
	Unnamed	Maritime (Search and Rescue)	Vietnam
	Unnamed	Counter-piracy	United States
	Cooperation Spirit 2012	HA/DR	Australia, New Zealand
	Unnamed	Counterterrorism	Jordan

APPENDIX II: CHINA AND TAIWAN FORCES DATA

Taiwan Strait Military Balance, Ground Forces			
	China		Taiwan
	Total	Taiwan Strait Area	Total
Personnel (Active)	1.25 million	400,000	130,000
Group Armies	18	8	3
Infantry Divisions	15	5	0
Infantry Brigades	16	6	8
Mechanized Infantry Divisions	6	2	0
Mechanized Infantry Brigades	17	7	3
Armor Divisions	1	0	0
Armor Brigades	16	7	4
Artillery Divisions	2	2	0
Artillery Brigades	17	6	5
Airborne Divisions	3	3	0
Amphibious Divisions	2	2	0
Amphibious Brigades	3	3	3
Tanks	7,000	3,000	1,100
Artillery Pieces	8,000	3,000	1,600

Note: PLA active ground forces are organized into group armies. Infantry, armor, and artillery units are organized into a combination of divisions and brigades deployed throughout the PLA's seven military regions (MRs). A significant portion of these assets are deployed in the Taiwan Strait area, specifically the Nanjing, Guangzhou, and Jinan MRs. Taiwan has seven defense commands, three of which have field armies. Each army contains an artillery command roughly equivalent to a brigade plus.

Taiwan Strait Military Balance, Naval Forces

| | China | | Taiwan |
	Total	East and South Sea Fleets	Total
Aircraft Carriers	1	0	0
Destroyers	23	16	4
Frigates	52	44	22
Tank Landing Ships/ Amphibious Transport Dock	29	27	12
Medium Landing Ships	26	24	4
Diesel Attack Submarines	49	33	4
Nuclear Attack Submarines	5	2	0
Coastal Patrol (Missile)	85	67	45

Note: The PLA Navy has the largest force of principal combatants, submarines, and amphibious warfare ships in Asia. In the event of a major Taiwan conflict, the East and South Sea Fleets would be expected to participate in direct action against the Taiwan Navy. The North Sea Fleet would be responsible primarily for protecting Beijing and the northern coast, but could provide mission-critical assets to support other fleets.

Taiwan Strait Military Balance, Air Forces

| | China | | Taiwan |
Aircraft	Total	Within range of Taiwan	Total
Fighters	1,700	330	388
Bombers/Attack	600	160	22
Transport	475	40	21

Note: The PLA Air Force and the PLA Navy have approximately 2,300 operational combat aircraft. These consist of air defense and multi-role fighters, ground attack aircraft, fighter-bombers, and bombers. An additional 1,450 older fighters, bombers and trainers are employed for training, research, and development. The two air arms also possess approximately 475 transports and more than 100 surveillance and reconnaissance aircraft with intelligence, surface search, and airborne early warning capabilities. The majority of PLA Air Force and PLA Navy aircraft are based in the eastern half of the country. Currently, 490 aircraft could conduct combat operations against Taiwan without refueling, but this number could be significantly increased through any combination of aircraft forward deployment, decreased ordnance loads, or altered mission profiles.

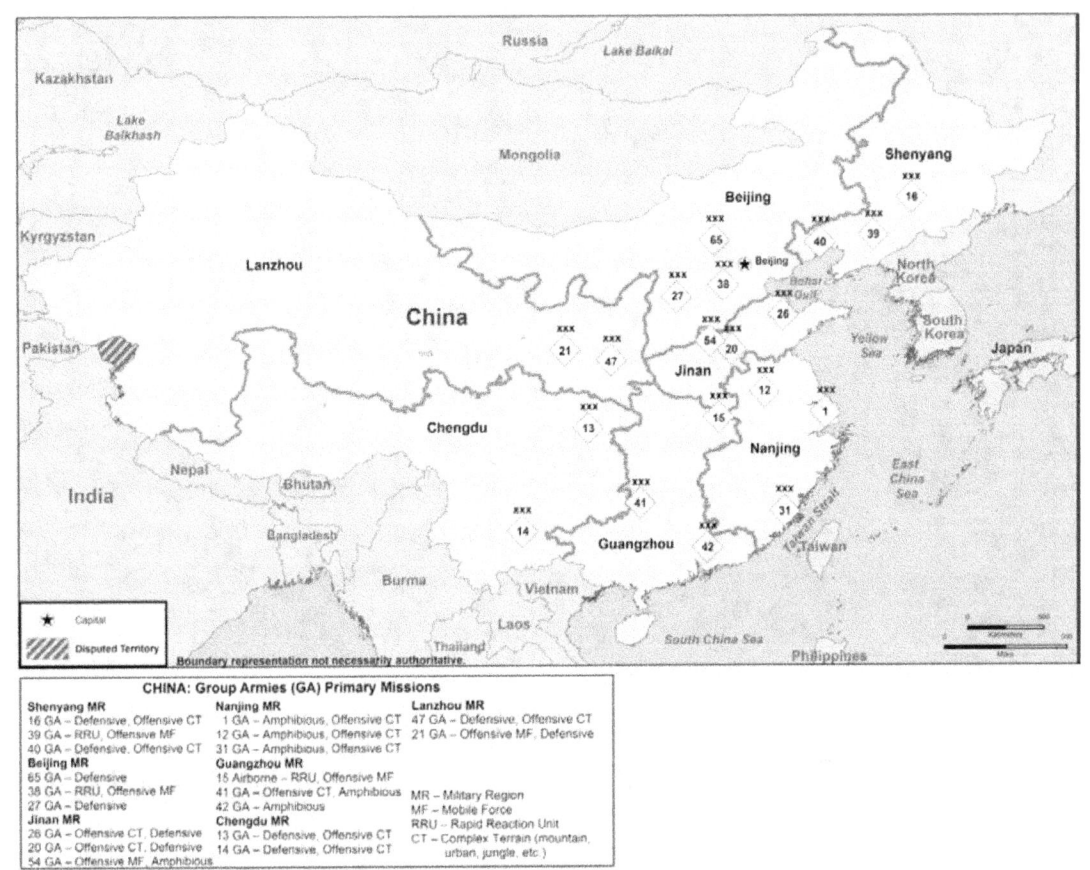

CHINA: Group Armies (GA) Primary Missions

Shenyang MR
16 GA – Defensive, Offensive CT
39 GA – RRU, Offensive MF
40 GA – Defensive, Offensive CT

Beijing MR
65 GA – Defensive
38 GA – RRU, Offensive MF
27 GA – Defensive

Jinan MR
26 GA – Offensive CT, Defensive
20 GA – Offensive CT, Defensive
54 GA – Offensive MF, Amphibious

Nanjing MR
1 GA – Amphibious, Offensive CT
12 GA – Amphibious, Offensive CT
31 GA – Amphibious, Offensive CT

Guangzhou MR
15 Airborne – RRU, Offensive MF
41 GA – Offensive CT, Amphibious
42 GA – Amphibious

Chengdu MR
13 GA – Defensive, Offensive CT
14 GA – Defensive, Offensive CT

Lanzhou MR
47 GA – Defensive, Offensive CT
21 GA – Offensive MF, Defensive

MR – Military Region
MF – Mobile Force
RRU – Rapid Reaction Unit
CT – Complex Terrain (mountain,
    urban, jungle, etc.)

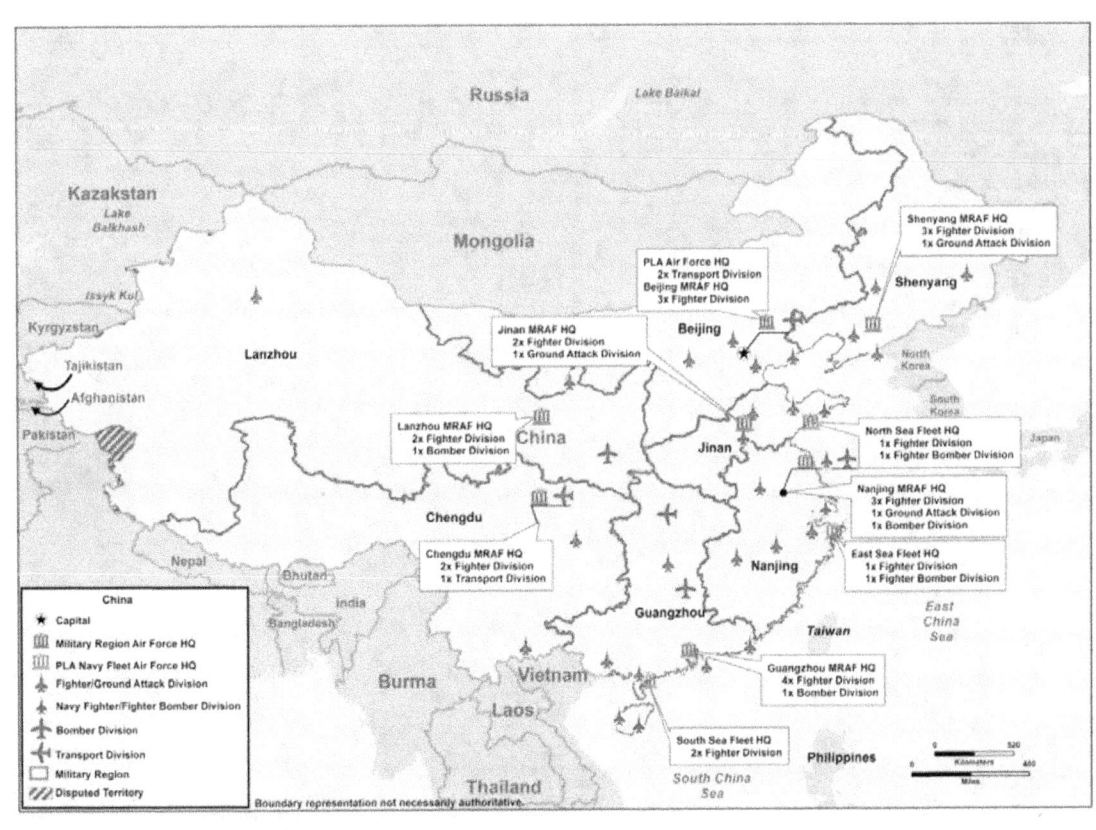

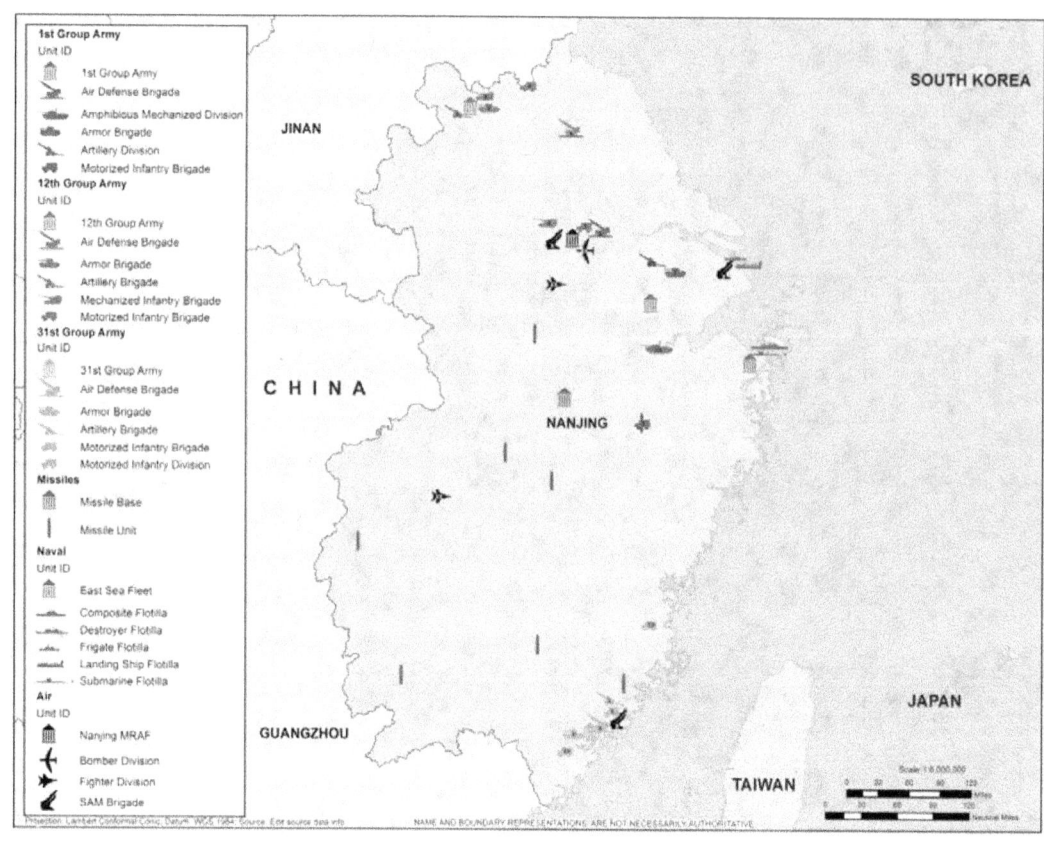

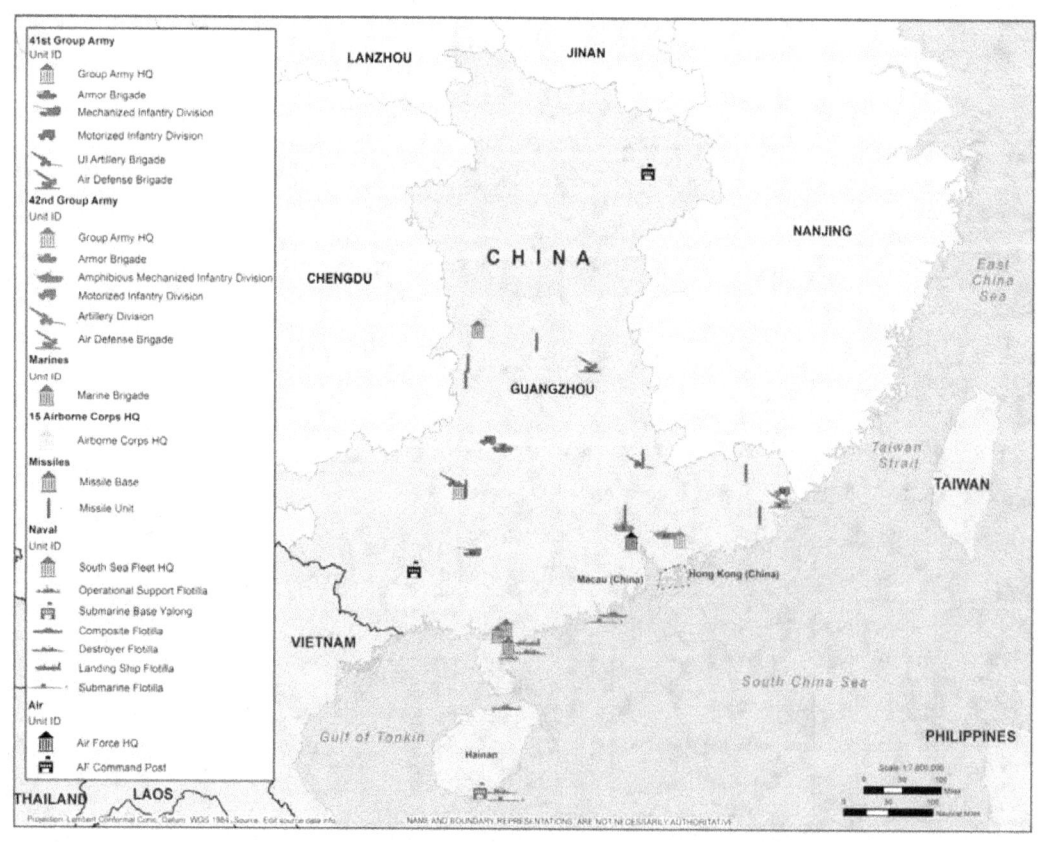

APPENDIX III: ADDITIONAL MAPS AND CHARTS

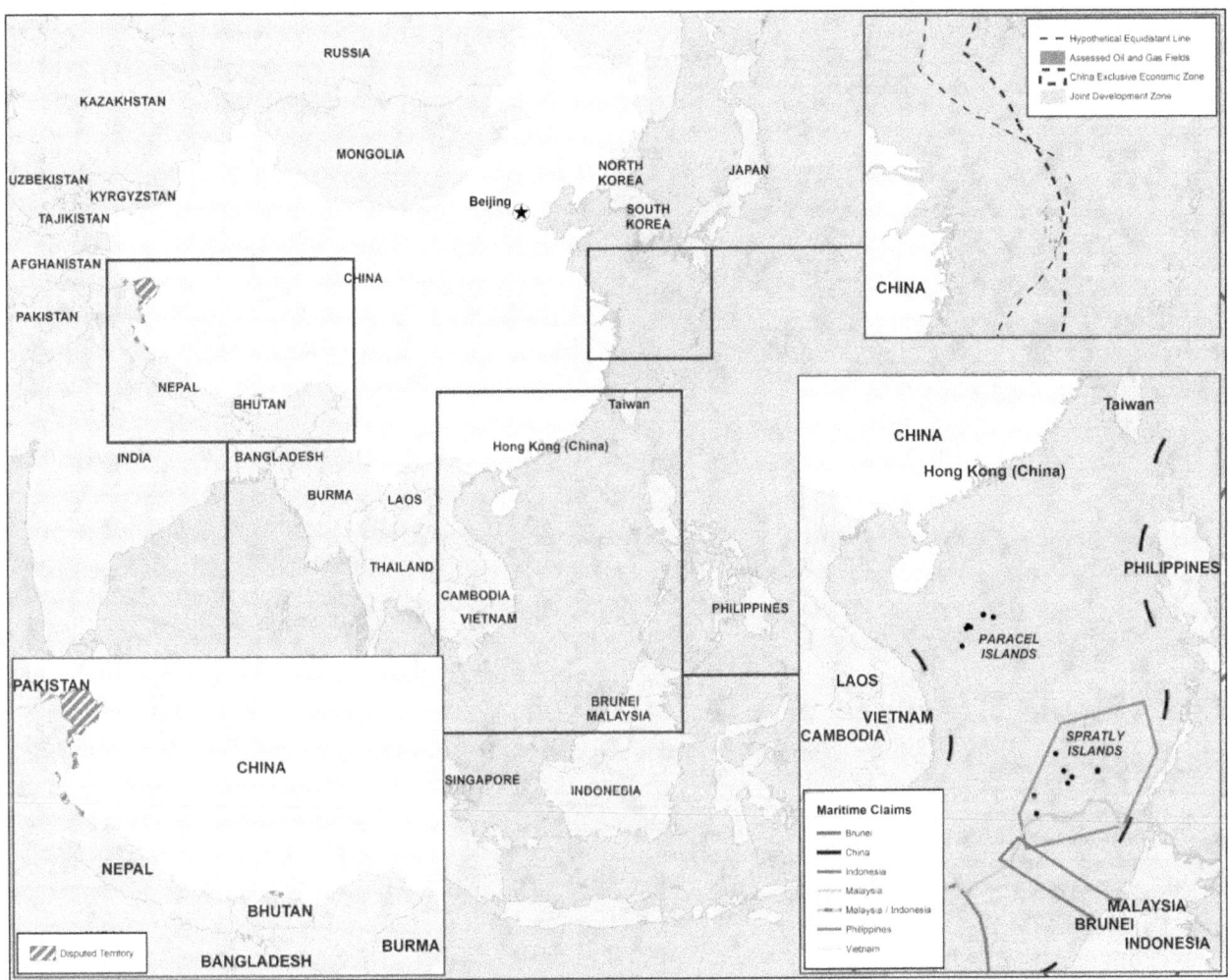

Figure 1: China's Sovereignty Claims

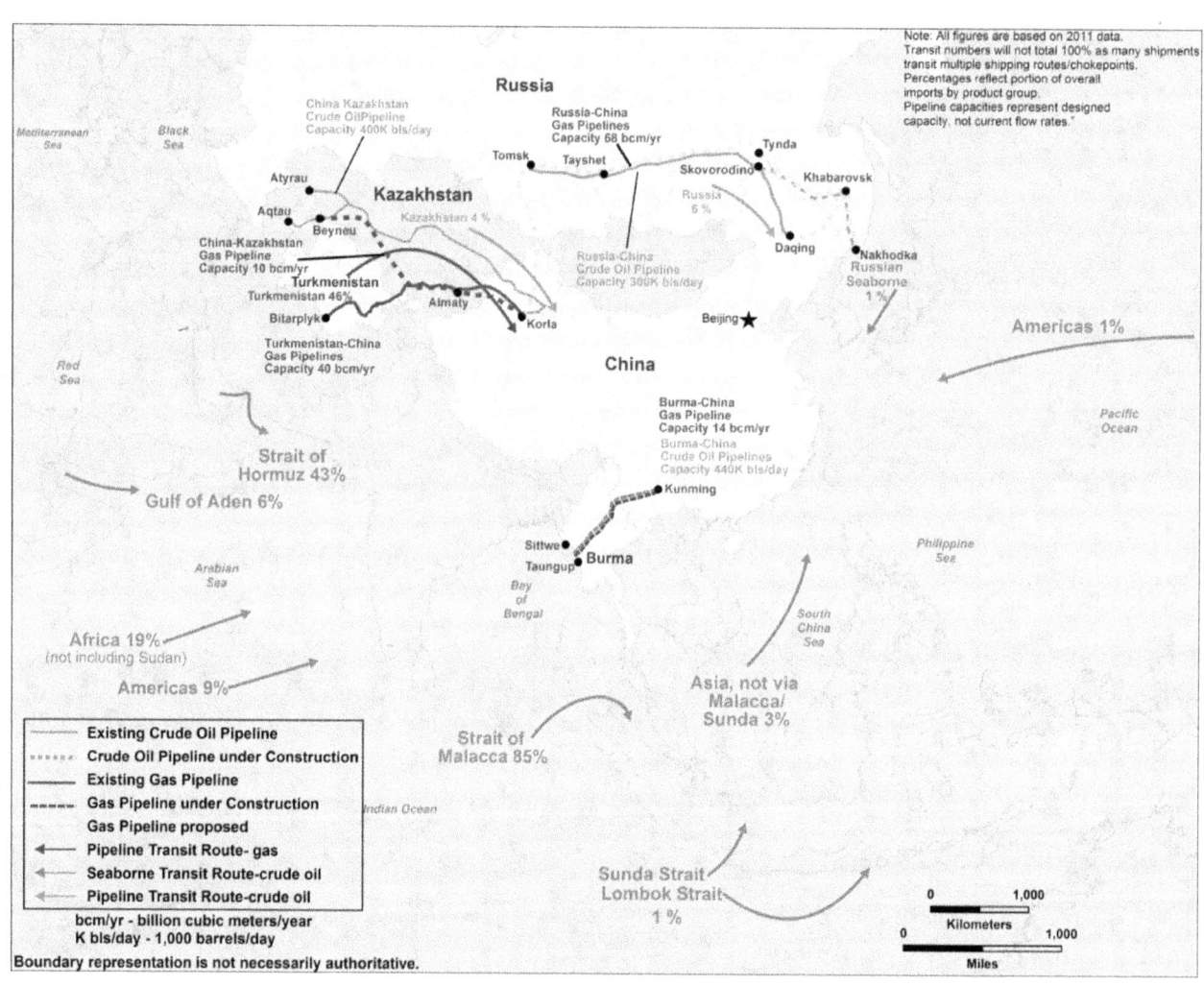

Figure 2: China's Import Transit Routes

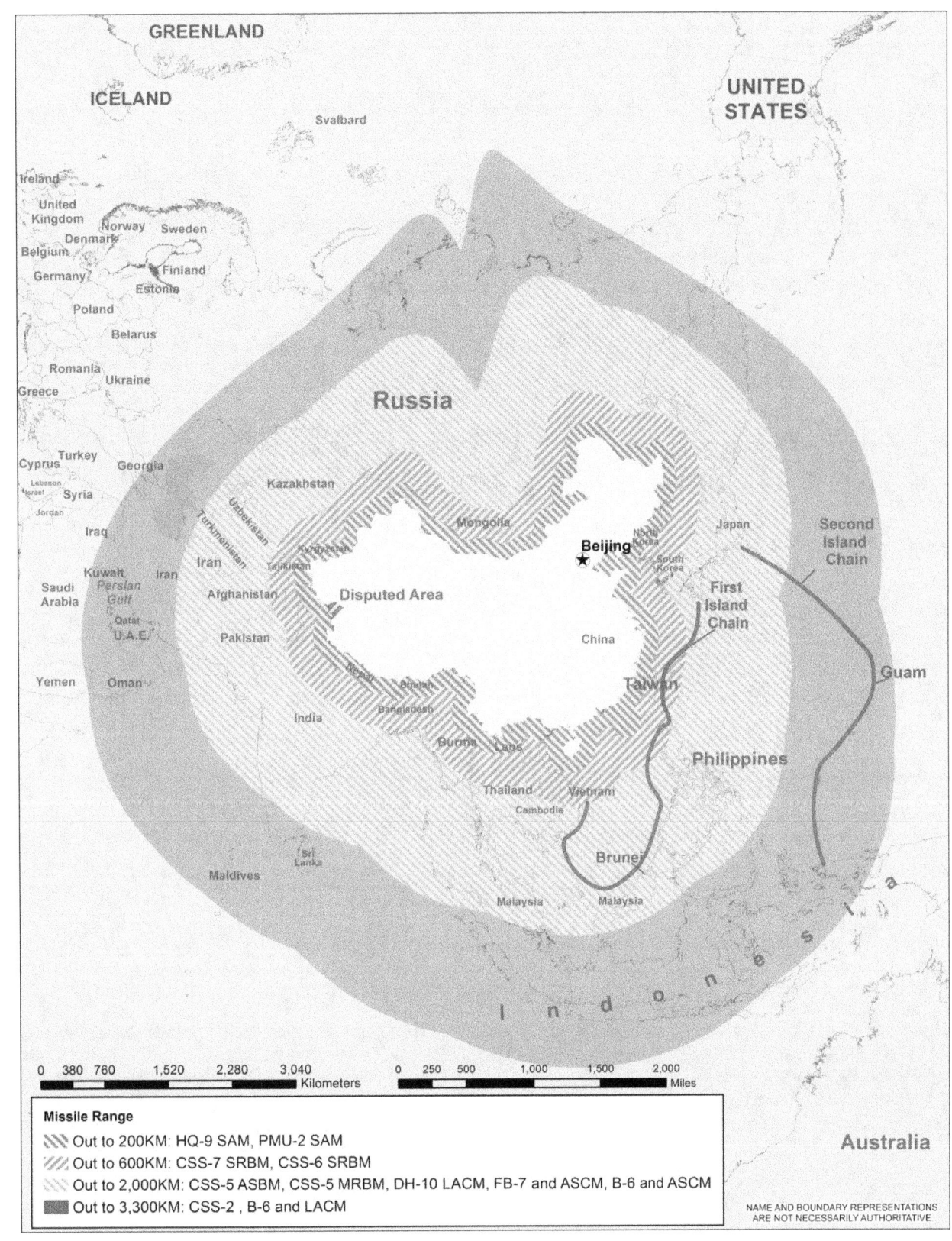

Figure 3: Conventional Strike Capabilities

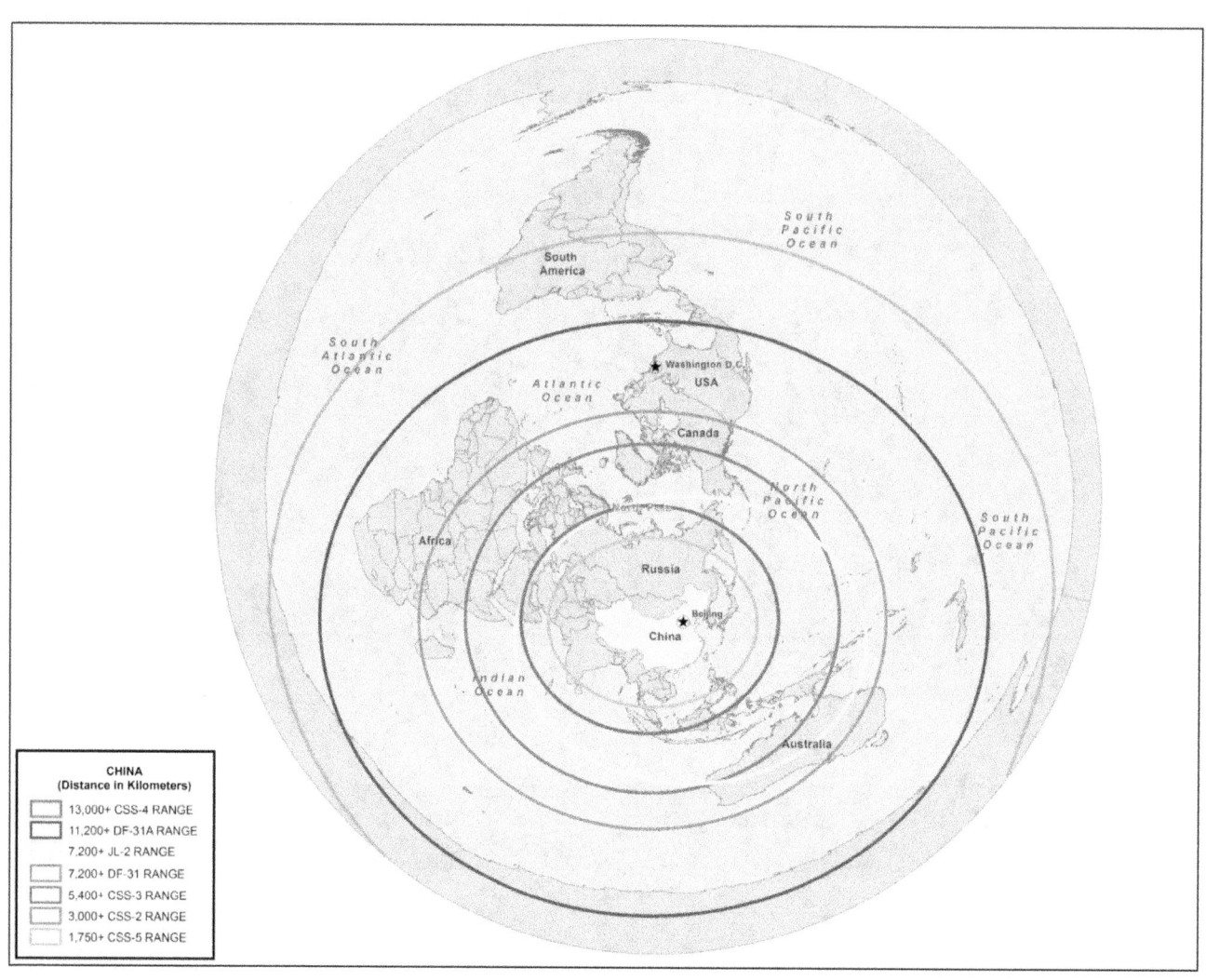

Figure 4: Medium and Intercontinental Range Ballistic Missiles

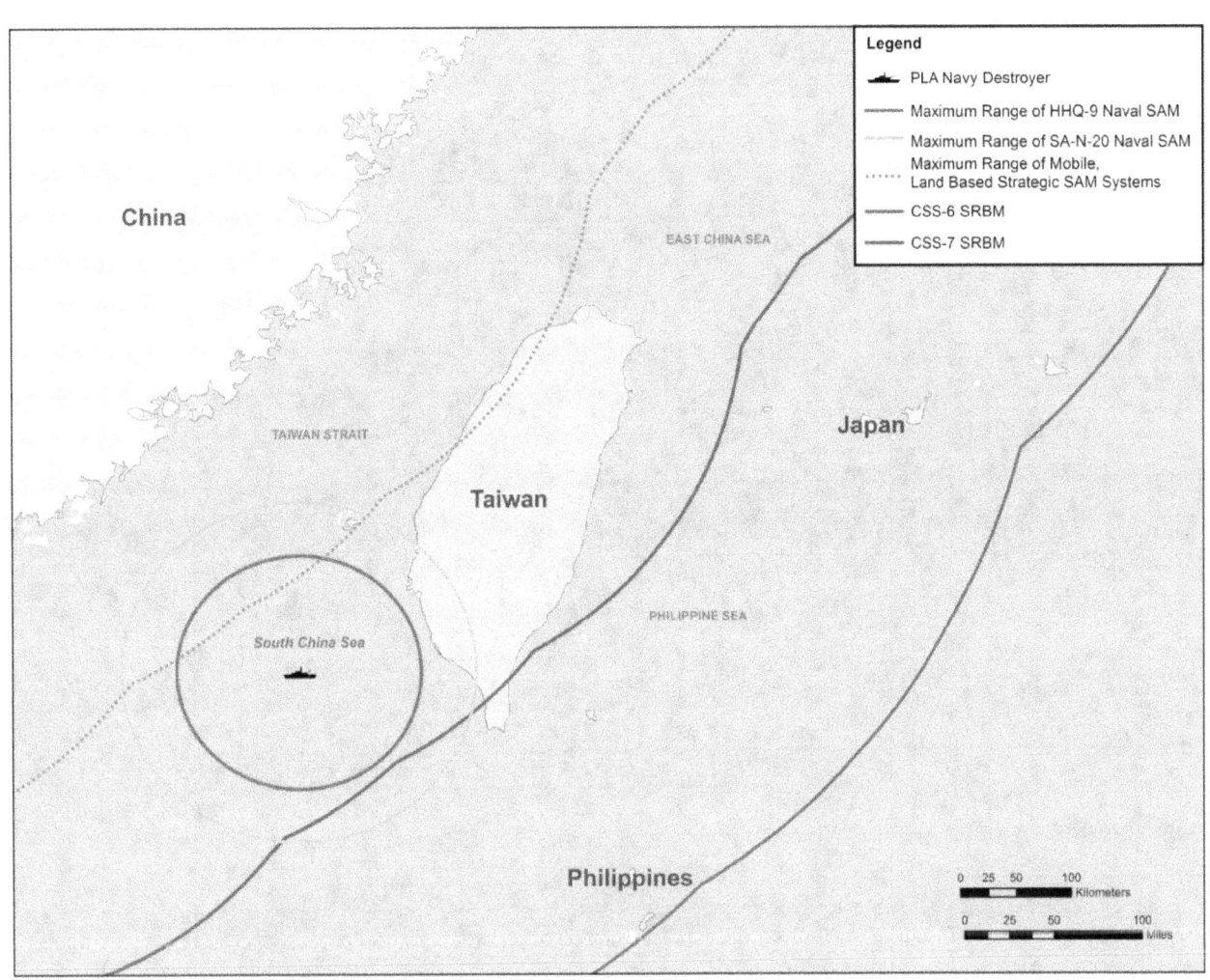

Figure 5: Taiwan Strait SAM and SRBM Coverage.

www.ingramcontent.com/pod-product-compliance
Lightning Source LLC
Chambersburg PA
CBHW080322290526
45790CB00005B/2152